EYEWITNESS
CIVIL WAR

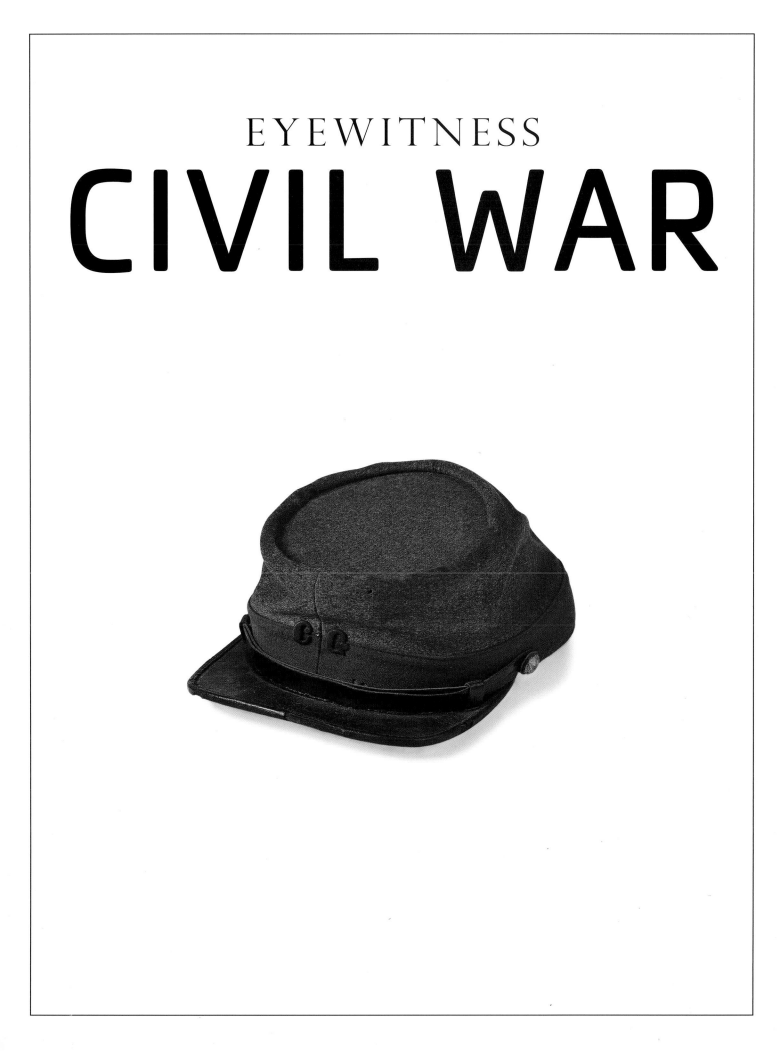

2nd Battalion flag,
Hilliard's Alabama Legion

Telescope

Canister
with lead slugs

Ketchum hand
grenade

Canteen and
haversack

Union private

EYEWITNESS
CIVIL WAR

Written by
JOHN STANCHAK

Model 1850
saber

Confederate currency

The Great Seal of the
Confederacy

Infantry drum

.44 caliber Colt
revolver

.58 caliber rifle

Jacket of
Rush's Lancers

Slave auction poster

Canvas-covered canteen

Confederate
General
Stand Watie

DK Penguin
Random
House

Publisher Neal Porter
Executive editor Iris Rosoff
Art director Dirk Kaufman
Project editor Andrea Curley
Designer Tom Carling, Carling Design, Inc.

RELAUNCH EDITION (DK UK)
Editor Ashwin Khurana
US editor Margaret Parrish
Managing editor Gareth Jones
Managing art editor Philip Letsu
Publisher Andrew Macintyre
Producer, pre-production Adam Stoneham
Senior producer Janis Griffith
Jacket editor Maud Whatley
Jacket designer Laura Brim
Jacket development manager Sophia MTT
Publishing director Jonathan Metcalf
Associate publishing director Liz Wheeler
Art director Phil Ormerod

RELAUNCH EDITION (DK INDIA)
Editor Ishani Nandi
Project art editor Deep Shikha Walia
Art editor Amit Varma
Senior DTP designer Harish Aggarwal
DTP designer Pawan Kumar
Managing editor Alka Thakur Hazarika
Managing art editor Romi Chakraborty
CTS manager Balwant Singh
Jacket designers Suhita Dharamjit, Šukriti Sobti
Managing jacket editor Saloni Singh

This American Edition, 2015
First American Edition, 2000

Published in the United States by DK Publishing
345 Hudson Street, New York, New York 10014

Copyright © 2000, © 2011, © 2015
Dorling Kindersley Limited
A Penguin Random House Company
Text copyright © 2000 by John Stanchak

15 16 17 18 19 10 9 8 7 6 5 4 3 2 1
01—274613—Mar/2015

A catalog record for this book is available
from the Library of Congress.
ISBN: 978-1-4654-3186-8 (PB)
ISBN: 978-1-4654-3360-2 (ALB)

DK books are available at special discounts when purchased
in bulk for sales promotions, premiums, fund-raising,
or educational use. For details, contact: DK Publishing Special
Markets, 345 Hudson Street, New York, New York 10014.
SpecialSales@dk.com

Printed in China by South China Printing Co Ltd, China
Color reproduction by Alta Image Ltd, London, UK

All images © Dorling Kindersley Limited
For further information see: www.dkimages.com

A WORLD OF IDEAS:
SEE ALL THERE IS TO KNOW

Confederate soldier

4th Regiment flag, Irish Brigade

Clara Barton

Contents

Writing implements
and letter

The long argument

An antislavery slogan
Americans who hated slavery formed organizations to try to end it. One group's slogan was the question "Am I Not a Man and a Brother?" These groups tried to force slave owners to admit that slaves were not farm property, but people like themselves.

By the mid 1800s, the issue of slavery had become a major cause of conflict in the United States. Slavery had long been outlawed in the industrialized northern states, but plantation owners in the agricultural South depended on slave labor. In the 1850s, fighting broke out between settlers in pro-slavery Missouri and their antislavery neighbors in Kansas. Missouri Border Ruffians rode across the state line to murder antislavery men. Kansas fighters, called Jayhawkers, retaliated. Eventually, the US Army was called out to take control. Some pro-slavery supporters called for Southern states to leave the Union, a process known as secession. In the years before the Civil War, these supporters of the secession campaign were known as Fire-Eaters.

More captives on the afterdeck

Half-starved captives

Leading Fire-Eater
Virginia farmer Edmund Ruffin believed the South had a different culture from the rest of America. In 1860, he helped South Carolinians organize their secession campaign. He had the honor of firing the cannon at Fort Sumter, South Carolina, that began the Civil War. After the conflict, he committed suicide rather than live under Union rule.

Saved from slavery
In 1807, it became illegal to import new slaves from Africa. However, slaves were still being smuggled into the South until the start of the Civil War. The people in this newspaper drawing were kidnapped in Africa in 1860. They were being shipped to America to be sold as slaves when they were rescued by US Navy sailors.

Unfinished city
In the months before the war, both the Capitol's dome and the Washington Monument in Washington, D.C. were still under construction. The capital was not an impressive place to work out the nation's problems.

Sumner was so badly injured that it took him years to recover from his injuries

SOUTHERN CHIVALRY — ARGUMENT VERSUS CLUB'S.

A very public beating

In 1856, Massachusetts attorney Charles Sumner stood on the floor of the Senate for two days speaking out against slavery and its supporters. One of the people he criticized was Andrew Butler, a senator from South Carolina. Butler was not present to reply. Two days later, however, his nephew, South Carolina Congressman Preston Brooks, strode into the Senate and beat Sumner senseless with a cane. South Carolinians applauded Brooks for defending his family's honor.

Cassy caring for Uncle Tom after his whipping

The book that fueled the flames

Harriet Beecher Stowe's novel *Uncle Tom's Cabin*, published in 1852, exposed the cruelty of slavery. It featured a wicked slave overseer named Simon Legree. This illustration features Uncle Tom, a kind but abused slave. The book became wildly popular in the North and was turned into an even more popular play.

Antislavery men of Kansas

This photo from the 1850s shows Kansas men ready to fight pro-slavery raiders from Missouri. At this time, violence over the slavery issue was at its peak. In Illinois, an antislavery newspaper publisher was lynched, while Southern law officers were beaten as they tried to capture runaway slaves in the North.

Slave life

By 1860, most white Americans were embarrassed by slavery. After the Revolutionary War and its promise that "all men are created equal," the states north of Maryland abolished slavery. But Southerners believed that without slaves their economy would be ruined. Because they could not explain how people could be slaves in a nation where all were supposed to be free, they simply called slavery the Peculiar Institution. While white men argued, black slaves suffered. They were paid nothing, fed little, and denied an education. They could be beaten or sold at any time. Long before the Civil War, slavery was a political and moral problem that would not go away.

Slaves who grew tired of hearing the copper bells muffled the clappers with dirt and mud

Slave collar

A slave collar
A slave could be worth several hundred dollars. If a slave seemed likely to run away, the master would lock him or her into this collar equipped with bells. As long as the master could hear the bells jingling, he knew his slave was close by.

Leg iron, which prevented a slave from bending the leg

Shackle

Tools of cruelty
This photograph was circulated throughout the North by antislavery activists. It shows a former slave posed in shackles and an iron collar to show some of the cruelties of slavery.

Auctioning slaves was a specialty for some of the auctioneering professionals

At work in the fields
These cotton workers are supervised by a mounted overseer, a white manager of slaves, employed by the plantation owner. Overseers were expected to discipline slaves and often gave out cruel punishments.

Slave auction
Slaves were sold at auctions. Before the auction, leaflets such as this were circulated. They described the men and women being put up for sale.

There was no one to care for young slave children, so they spent time in the fields from birth

Auctioneer

Slave handler

Slave buyer

Overseer

Slaves for sale

The Peculiar Institution was a business in which millions of dollars could be made. This painting of a slave auction is from 1852. The last public slave auction in the US was held in Missouri in 1865.

Canvas cotton sack

King cotton

These are picked bolls of raw cotton. In 1793, Eli Whitney of New England invented the cotton gin, a hand-cranked machine that combed and seeded cotton in large quantities. This made cotton the "king" of the Southern economy, and created a need for tens of thousands of slaves to work the cotton fields.

Cotton boll

The election of 1860

In the presidential election of 1860, slavery was the main topic of debate. The Constitution Party said slavery and the Constitution should be left as they were. The Democratic Party split into two groups—those who supported slavery and those who wanted a compromise. The six-year-old Republican Party opposed slavery. Its candidate was Illinois attorney Abraham Lincoln, a man with little experience in government. Lincoln won the election. His opponents were outraged; some even demanded that the election be declared invalid and repeated. Pro-slavery Americans were expected to accept a leader they did not want. They took radical action instead.

Candidate Lincoln
In Lincoln's time, presidential candidates did not make many personal appearances. Their supporters did the traveling and made the speeches. Printed portraits of the candidates were posted on walls or passed around to friends. Several candidates embraced new technology and distributed photographs of themselves. Lincoln, however, was not regarded as a handsome man, and pictures of him were rarely seen. Many people who voted for Lincoln had no idea what he looked like.

Parade torch
In the middle 1800s, supporters of all parties held rallies for their candidates. Since these events often took place at night, marchers carried parade torches like this one. The flames lit the way for candidates, supporters, and marching bands as they walked through towns and villages chanting campaign slogans.

Angel of the Union, overseeing all

A winning pair
This Republican poster from 1860 shows Lincoln's running mate, US Senator Hannibal Hamlin of Maine. Hamlin was expected to appeal to the Northeastern voters. But the political climate changed. In 1864, the party replaced him with Andrew Johnson, a Union loyalist from Tennessee.

Symbol of Freedom

LINCOLN.

HAMLIN.

Symbol of Agriculture

Symbol of Industry

Symbol of Justice

In the 1860 election, Douglas received 1,375,000 votes to Lincoln's 1,866,000. He died eight months after the election. In his last days, he asked all Americans to support Lincoln and the Union

Candidate Douglas
Democrat Stephen Douglas was a famous politician in 1860. He was a skilled speaker and a likable man. In 1858, Abraham Lincoln ran against him for his Senate seat, debating him in public several times. Although Lincoln lost that election, the debates introduced the little-known politician to the American public.

Candidate Breckinridge
Democrat John C. Breckinridge served as vice president during President James Buchanan's term in office. Breckinridge was a Democrat from Kentucky, a slave state. After losing the 1860 election to Lincoln, Breckinridge became a Confederate general.

The abolitionists

Slave stealer
Abolitionist Captain J. Walker was arrested at Key West, Florida, in the 1850s with a boatload of escaped slaves. He was jailed and branded on the palm of his right hand with the letters SS. The letters stood for "slave stealer."

White opponents of slavery, called abolitionists, organized their resistance in the 1820s and 1830s. Early leaders were clergymen and Quakers, members of a religious group who opposed violence. In 1826, Levi Coffin, a Quaker from North Carolina, set up an operation in Ohio known as the Underground Railroad. This was a system of secret trails that ran from the northernmost slave states, through New England, to Canada. Escaped slaves linked up with guides, called conductors, who led the escapees along the trails. At its best, the Railroad freed only about a thousand slaves a year. But its very existence, and the silent cooperation of thousands of Northerners, angered slave owners greatly.

An abolitionist fanatic
John Brown was a farmer and abolitionist from Ohio. In October, 1859, with the help of armed associates, he attacked the town and government arms factory at Harpers Ferry. Brown hoped to arm slaves with guns from the arsenal and start a rebellion. He believed God wanted him to end slavery with bloodshed. After his arrest, his attorneys wanted him to plead insanity. Brown refused.

The Harpers Ferry engine house became a tourist attraction in the days following the crisis and was photographed often. This souvenir picture is from the postwar years

A strategic location
Harpers Ferry lies at the end of a valley, where the Shenandoah and Potomac Rivers meet. Because the town sits beside waters that could power machinery, it was chosen as the site for a US government arms factory. It was a good target not only for John Brown in 1859, but also for warring Civil War generals two years later.

John Brown's fort
When John Brown and his gang attacked Harpers Ferry, they took several prominent citizens hostage. Armed with weapons, they barricaded themselves inside the local fire company's engine house. Within two days, a small force of US Marines arrived and smashed open the engine house door. All the Marines escaped harm, but Brown was wounded and arrested. He was tried, convicted of treason, and executed.

Frederick Douglass
The best-known antislavery spokesperson of the prewar years was Frederick Douglass, the son of a plantation slave woman and her white master. As a young man, he obtained forged papers and traveled north by railroad to freedom. After receiving an education, he became a forceful speaker on the abolitionist circuit and wrote a best-selling autobiography that described the heartbreak of slavery.

General Tubman
Harriet Tubman was a Maryland field slave who escaped to Philadelphia and became a famous conductor on the Underground Railroad. The slaves she led to freedom in the years before the Civil War nicknamed her Moses. John Brown knew her and called her General Tubman. After becoming a national celebrity, Tubman died in 1913, at the age of 92.

A life devoted to the cause of freedom
Sojourner Truth was born a slave in New York State around 1797. In 1827, she escaped and took refuge with an abolitionist family named Van Wagener. In 1843, after claiming to have heard divine voices, she changed her name and began lecturing on abolitionism. She dictated her life story to writer Olive Gilbert, and her book, *Narrative of Sojourner Truth*, became a best-seller. The money she earned from her book sales helped fund the work of the Underground Railroad.

An important headline
On December 20, 1860, this headline from the *Charleston Mercury* informed the people of Charleston of the vote for secession even before the news had reached Washington, D.C.

The Great Seal
This is a pewter copy of the Great Seal of the Confederacy, the official stamp of the young Confederate government.

Secession

Pro-slavery Southerners were angry at the election of Abraham Lincoln. In South Carolina, voters called for the state's secession from the Union. In December, 1860, South Carolina declared its independence from the United States. Militiamen there seized US government property. Major Robert Anderson took a small force into Fort Sumter on an island in Charleston Harbor. He was determined to save this bit of US property. South Carolinians were equally determined to take the fort. For three months they surrounded the harbor with heavy cannons. During this time, other states seceded. In March, 1861 in Montgomery, Alabama, these seceded states formed a new government—the Confederate States of America. On April 11, Confederate cannons fired on Fort Sumter. These shots began the Civil War.

Alexander Stephens
The forgotten vice president of the Confederate States of America was Alexander Stephens of Georgia. Small, thin, and sickly, Stephens came to be known as Little Aleck.

Jefferson Davis
In March, 1861, Jefferson Davis was named president of the Confederate States. This was a temporary appointment. Later, in February, 1862, Davis stood for the national election and was chosen by the Southern people to serve a six-year term. This formal portrait of him was made long afterwards.

Secession Hall
Charleston citizens were jubilant when state representatives voted their state out of the Union. The vote was taken at an auditorium called Institute Hall. The spot was later named Secession Hall.

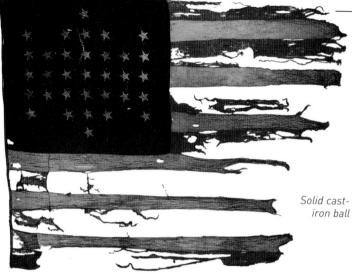

A flag of Fort Sumter

This small flag flew over the fort during its bombardment. It was knocked down by a Confederate shell early on April 12, 1861. Under fire, a Union sergeant climbed the flagpole and nailed it back into place.

Cannons and guns

This cannonball was fired during the duel between Fort Sumter's cannons and Confederate guns around Charleston Harbor. No one on either side was killed by artillery fire during the fight.

Solid cast-iron ball

FIRED FROM FORT MOULTRIE, INTO CHARLESTON, S.C. 1861

This Confederate cannonball was intended for Fort Sumter. It landed in Charleston instead.

Souvenir

After the surrender of Sumter, Southerners celebrated by carrying away pieces of the fort as mementos. A piece of the Union flagstaff was cut, polished, and made into a cane for General Pierre Gustave Toutant Beauregard, the leader of the Southern force at Sumter.

Surrender of Fort Sumter

Confederate troops fired on Fort Sumter on April 11, 1861. Major Robert Anderson, his 85 soldiers, and 43 laborers fought back with cannons, but eventually lowered their flag on the afternoon of April 12.

Raising armies

When President Lincoln heard that Fort Sumter had surrendered, he called for 75,000 militia troops to protect Washington, D.C. Over the coming years, both Abraham Lincoln and Jefferson Davis asked for volunteers every few months. In 1862, the Confederate Congress approved conscription—the drafting of men into the army. The US Congress did the same in 1863. Many people objected to the draft and there were riots in New York in 1863. But in the end, both sides put millions of soldiers in the field.

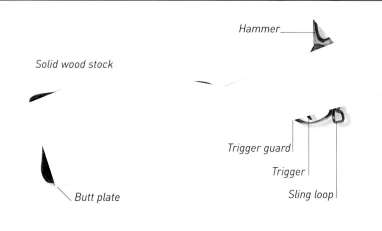

Solid wood stock

Hammer

Trigger guard

Trigger

Butt plate

Sling loop

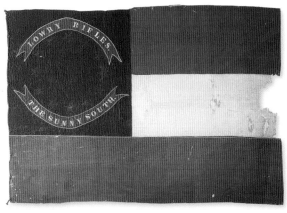

The sunny South
Mississippi, the second state to secede, sent 80,000 men into the army. This is the flag of one of the state's early volunteer units, the Lowry Rifles. Its men showed regional pride by adopting the motto "The Sunny South" for their flag.

Homemade uniforms
Many of the uniforms were handmade at home. The sister of Private James Lampton of Mississippi made this hat for him out of pine straw.

7th Regiment
When Lincoln called for 75,000 troops, New York City sent its 7th Regiment. Here, people cheer as the men march to the train bound for Washington.

Bounty money
Many disliked the way some regiments recruited. Criminals called "bounty jumpers" would join up to receive bounty money, then desert the army. Later, they used an alias to join another regiment.

Spout

Stamped tin

A standard rifle

Both the Union and Confederate armies used versions of this .58 caliber rifle. In the North, it was called the Springfield Model 1861 after the armory where it was first made. The model shown here was made in Richmond, Virginia, for Southern troops.

Rear sight   Barrel band   Forged steel barrel   Blade sight

A recruiting poster

Government officials recruited volunteers with posters. These were hung in town squares, open-air markets, and on the fronts of stores and newspaper offices. This enlistment poster was one of the most popular types seen in the first days of the Civil War. It gives the impression that the war will be an adventure.

Very basic equipment

Water was very important to the Civil War soldier. In summer, men were lost on marches because of dehydration. Many of the first volunteers were given tin canteens, like this one above.

Everyone's war

In the 1860s, some groups of people were discouraged from joining the Union and Confederate armies. Native Americans were excluded from many volunteer regiments and, in the Northeast, there was a lot of prejudice against members of immigrant groups. Men from these minorities formed their own volunteer regiments. Irishmen, Jews, Italians, and Germans enlisted in units made up of other patriotic immigrants. Native Americans fought in "Indian outfits" in both armies. The adventure of the Civil War also attracted professional soldiers from other countries, who were called foreign observers.

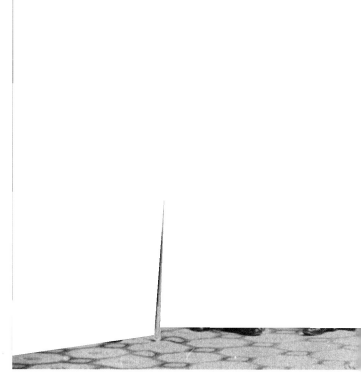

Italian volunteers
Italian-born members of New York City's Garibaldi Guard wore uniforms that let everyone know their country of origin. Their broad-brimmed hats were decorated with rooster feathers. Such feathers are considered emblems of courage and are still worn on Italian military caps.

Marcus Spiegel
Most members of the 120th Regiment of Ohio Volunteers were Protestant. Their colonel, Marcus Spiegel, however, was a Jewish businessman with excellent leadership skills. The 120th saw hard combat during the siege of Vicksburg, Mississippi.

Irish troops at Mass
In the 1860s, most Americans were Protestant and were wary of different faiths. The Irish troops in this photograph had a Catholic priest as their chaplain. But members of one largely Jewish regiment in the Union army were not allowed to have a rabbi as their spiritual leader. The war was nearly over before the Northern army changed its rules.

Austro-Hungarian-style uniform coat

A man of influence

Judah Benjamin was the only Jewish member of Confederate President Jefferson Davis's cabinet. He served as the Confederacy's secretary of state, and briefly as secretary of war. In that role, Benjamin's decisions affected the lives of all Confederate soldiers.

The Irishman from Arkansas

Patrick R. Cleburne was born in Ireland and immigrated to Arkansas. In the Confederate army, he rose to the rank of major general and led his troops to many victories. Cleburne was killed in November, 1864, at the Battle of Franklin, Tennessee. He was shot while shouting for his men to follow him in a charge.

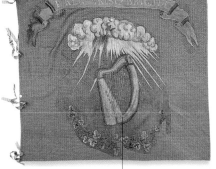

Easy target

Irish-born Union Brigadier General T. F. Meagher raised a brigade of Irish immigrant volunteers. Each regiment in the brigade carried one of these banners. However, the green banners made good targets for Southern bullets.

Irish harp

Game of dominoes

European observers

This photograph shows three titled French military men, the Duc de Chartes, the Prince de Joinville, and the Comte de Paris. They all served with Union Major General George McClellan's staff in 1862.

A chief and a general

Stand Watie was a chief of the Cherokee tribe in what is today Oklahoma. He formed a brigade of Native Americans to fight for the South and was made a brigadier general. In June, 1865, Watie was the last Confederate general to surrender his troops.

Muzzle-loading rifle

Side knife

German brothers

George and Herman Grothe, from Illinois, were born in Germany. They both served in regiments in the Midwest.

Women at war

In the 1860s, around the globe, laws and customs prohibited women from taking part in war. But in the US, there was a different attitude. For generations, women had supported their men in wars against the British, Mexicans, and Native Americans. When the men went off to battle, the women stayed behind to look after farms, businesses, and communities. Though their numbers were small, women played a role in

Union and Confederate government departments. While most army nurses were men, women were allowed to serve as hospital volunteers. In the North, many women belonged to the Sanitary Commission. This was an organization that traveled to the field with supplies for soldier relief.

A Confederate angel
Phoebe Pember is known for her selfless work in Confederate army hospitals in Virginia. After the war, she published a journal of her hospital experiences. It criticized the Southern government's administration of its hospitals.

A union patriot
Clara Barton is remembered as the founder of the American Red Cross. During the Civil War, she won fame as a battlefield nursing volunteer. Throughout the conflict, Clara Barton frequently risked her life to help the sick and wounded.

Supporting the troops
These women from the Philadelphia Academy of Fine Arts are sewing a flag for Union army volunteers.

Crutch

Medicine bottle

Hospital nursing

Northern female nursing volunteers were eventually organized by medical reformer, Dorothea Dix. However, they were not allowed to serve near the front lines. Like the volunteer shown here, female nurses were confined to supervised service in hospitals.

Loreta Velázquez

Tall tale?

Loreta Velázquez was a Southerner of Cuban-American descent. She claimed to have served in the Confederate army as Lieutenant Harry Buford so that she could be near her soldier-husband. She also claimed to have worked as a spy. Most veterans found Madame Velázquez's claims outrageous. Yet the memoirs she wrote after the war, titled *The Woman in Battle*, sold well.

A genuine army volunteer

Canadian Sarah Edmonds was working in the United States when the Civil War broke out. Disguised as a man, she joined a Union army regiment and served without being detected until she became ill. Rather than be found out by an army doctor, Sarah Edmonds deserted the army.

Velázquez disguised as a man

Refugees in flight

When warring armies passed through communities, women and children often became refugees. The woman below was displaced with her children when Union troops evicted all civilians from her county.

Sun bonnet

Quilt

Furniture

Gingham dress

Young and old

Throughout history, there have been famous old soldiers and very brave young ones. When the Civil War broke out, 74-year-old Lieutenant General Winfield Scott led the Union army. He was in poor health and had trouble sitting on a horse. But before leaving the army in November, 1861, he developed a broad military strategy that later led to Union victory. For his part, John Clem of Ohio won national attention when, as a 10-year-old, he survived the vicious combat at the Battle of Shiloh, Tennessee. But he was not the only extremely young volunteer. More than 3,900 boys, aged 16 and under, wrangled their way into the Union army, and it is estimated that there were even more boy soldiers serving the Confederacy.

The wounded drummer boy
This romanticized painting of a wounded young drummer being carried on the shoulder of an older soldier was popular after the war.

An elderly Union veteran
Winfield Scott was America's most honored soldier at the start of the Civil War. He joined the army in 1808, led troops in the War of 1812, commanded the forces that conquered Mexico City in 1848, and was the Whig Party's presidential candidate in 1852. Though born and raised in pro-slave Virginia, he stood by the Union. He died in 1866.

Major General Twiggs
Northerners called 71-year-old David Twiggs a traitor. In 1861, Major General Twiggs, a native of Georgia, commanded the US forces in Texas. When Texas seceded from the Union, he surrendered all its US forts to local Confederates and turned over all army supplies and payrolls to Southern authorities. His reward was a Confederate general's commission.

Epaulet

The belt plate shows the Georgia coat of arms

Father and son soldiers
Volunteers who made up the first militia companies often came from small towns and neighborhoods. It was common for brothers, or fathers and sons, to volunteer together. This Southern father and son posed together for the camera before heading off to war.

Boy soldier's souvenir
Landon Creek was very young when he joined a regiment of Mississippi volunteers. He was wounded three times before he turned 15. After the war he became a doctor. But he always kept this small hat to remind him of his days as a boy soldier.

White patent-leather cross belt

Gray wool tunic

Noncommissioned officer's dress sword

Drummer boy
John Clem ran away from his Ohio home to join the army at the age of nine. He had turned 10 by the time he served at the Battle of Shiloh. In 1863, at the Battle of Chickamauga, in Georgia, Clem shot a Southern officer who tried to force him to surrender. Clem retired from the US Army as a major general in 1916.

Underage
Many young volunteers wrote the number 18 on a piece of paper, then stuffed the paper into their shoe. When asked if they were over 18, the boys believed that they could say "yes" without having to lie since they were "over" the paper marked with "18."

Cap box

Home from home
At the start of the war, every foot soldier had a waterproof leather knapsack and blanket roll. The bag contained spare clothing, eating utensils, extra ammunition, and personal items. Later, many soldiers abandoned these sacks and carried their possessions in a simple blanket roll over their shoulders.

Outfitting armies

When nations go to war, they must make sure factories produce clothing and equipment for their soldiers for as long as the fighting lasts. During the Civil War, factories in the North did just that, producing blue wool uniforms, rifles, pistols, swords, ammunition, and camp equipment, as well as tools to repair these things. In the Confederate states, there were fewer factories, so the South's soldiers had to make do with homemade uniforms and weapons imported from Europe. When these things wore out or broke, there was little or nothing with which to replace them.

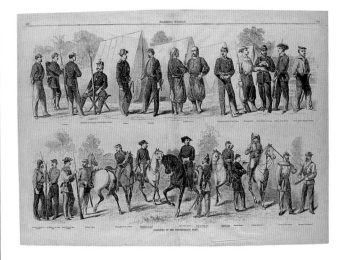

Confederate uniforms
Early in the war, many Southern troops wore attractive uniforms, made at home or by tailors. These pages from *Harper's Weekly* in 1861 show the variety of uniforms worn by some Confederate regiments.

Canvas canteen cover

Carrying food and drink
Infantrymen carried their water in canvas-covered canteens. Personal items and food rations were carried in haversacks—bags slung across the shoulder on a strap.

For cut and thrust
This fighting blade, called a Model 1850, was carried by both Union and Confederate infantry officers. Many of these swords were taken home as souvenirs after the conflict.

Grip *Brass hilt*

Barrel lug

Appearances are deceiving
Some regiments used sword bayonets. While they looked frightening at the end of a rifle, they were expensive to make and awkward to carry.

Brass hand guard *Hammer* *Collapsing rear sight* *Iron barrel* *Front blade sight*

Trigger *Sling loop* *Ramrod*

Walnut shoulder stock *Sling loop*

Dependable in battle
First called the Mississippi Rifle and later the Harpers Ferry Rifle, the single-shot .54 caliber US Model 1841 rifle was the standard weapon of the US Army at the start of the Civil War. With a 33-inch barrel, it proved itself a powerful weapon.

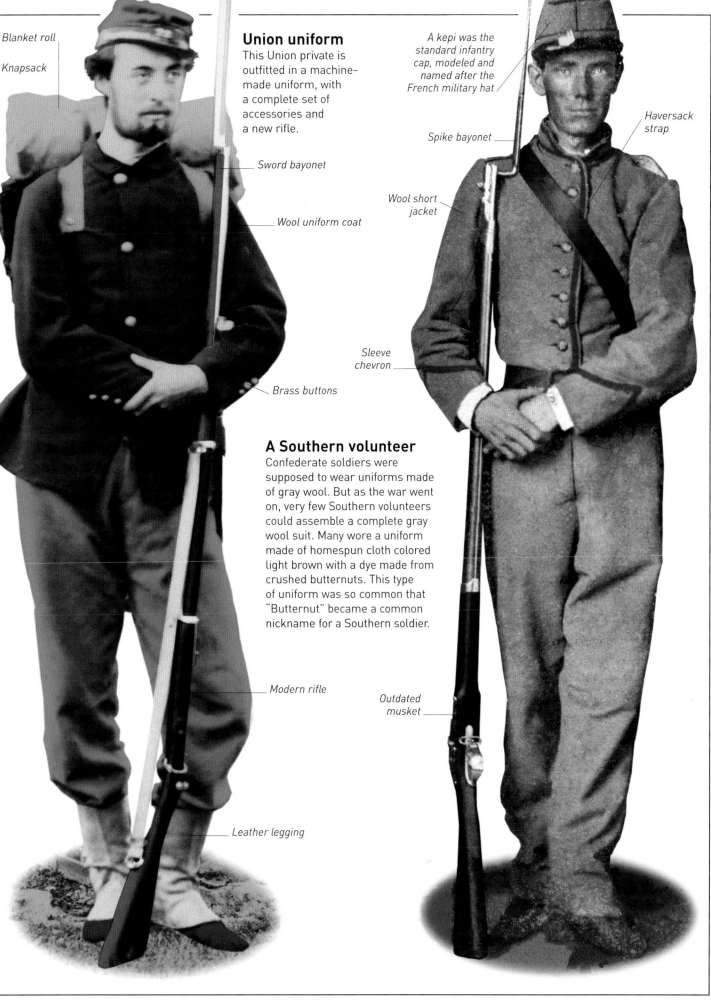

Blanket roll

Knapsack

Union uniform
This Union private is
outfitted in a machine-
made uniform, with
a complete set of
accessories and
a new rifle.

Sword bayonet

Wool uniform coat

Brass buttons

A kepi was the
standard infantry
cap, modeled and
named after the
French military hat

Spike bayonet

Haversack
strap

Wool short
jacket

Sleeve
chevron

A Southern volunteer
Confederate soldiers were
supposed to wear uniforms made
of gray wool. But as the war went
on, very few Southern volunteers
could assemble a complete gray
wool suit. Many wore a uniform
made of homespun cloth colored
light brown with a dye made from
crushed butternuts. This type
of uniform was so common that
"Butternut" became a common
nickname for a Southern soldier.

Modern rifle

Outdated
musket

Leather legging

Bull Run

Troops riding atop boxcars

Near Washington, D.C. is Manassas, Virginia. A stream nearby is named Bull Run. The fields around the stream were the sites of two major Civil War fights. The First Battle of Bull Run took place on July 21, 1861. Confederate General Beauregard had an army of 20,000 men at Manassas, while Union Brigadier General Irvin McDowell had brought more than 30,000 troops. Many local residents rode out to the fields to watch the conflict. The fight started at dawn on July 21. After a few hours, Beauregard's men received reinforcements, who helped to drive the Union soldiers from the field. As they retreated, they were shelled. The frightened civilians fled, creating a traffic jam that panicked McDowell's troops. Many dropped their weapons and ran for safety.

Taking the train to battle
Troops led by Confederate General Joseph Johnston boarded railroad trains in Virginia and arrived at the Bull Run battlefield in time to reinforce Beauregard's forces.

McDowell
General Irvin McDowell is the officer on the left in this photograph. Bull Run was the only large-scale battle where McDowell commanded the Union forces. Later, in 1861, George McClellan, on the right, would lead the Northern army.

A limber, a field artillery ammunition chest

Gray uniform   *Blanket roll*   *Sword bayonet*

Assorted uniforms
Clothing was a problem for both armies at Bull Run. Some Northerners wore gray uniforms. Some Southerners wore blue uniforms. Others, such as the Zouave regiment, modeled their uniforms on the gaudy clothes of the Zouava tribe of Algeria in Africa. The lack of standard uniforms created deadly confusion on the battlefield.

Union volunteer of the 7th New York Regiment

Garibaldi Guard member in an Italian army hat

New York volunteer of the Fire Zouave Regiment

Legging

Newspaper artist

Irish flag of the
69th New York

Havelock, a covering worn
as protection from the sun

National flag of
the Confederacy

Knapsack

One of many who
fought in shirtsleeves

Iron bayonet

Corcoran

The 69th New York regiment was a group of volunteer soldiers. Many of them were Irish immigrants. They carried a green flag decorated with the Irish harp. The 69th's colonel, Michael Corcoran (seen here on his horse), was captured during this battle. He was exchanged for Confederate prisoners and later became a brigadier general.

Beauregard

General P. G. T. Beauregard led the main Confederate army in the First Battle of Bull Run. His success in capturing Fort Sumter in April, 1861, led to Beauregard being appointed one of the highest-ranking generals of the Confederacy.

Epaulets

These brass epaulets were worn on the shoulders of General Beauregard's dress uniform. They were kept in a large, hard, leather case.

General's stars

Distracted

In this newspaper drawing done on-site, civilians are seen talking to and distracting some of the officers. The presence of townspeople at the battle caused problems and confusion for the soldiers.

Civilian

Racing away from defeat

This painting shows the Union army's panicked retreat from Bull Run. A Confederate shell hit Union wagons on a narrow bridge and blocked the way. Union soldiers felt trapped. Instead of marching from the battlefield in an orderly way, they threw down their equipment and ran for their lives.

Medical treatment

Souvenir
Confederate Major D. C. Merwin had his right arm amputated after being wounded in battle. This is the jacket he wore that day. Merwin saved it as a souvenir, along with a pair of left-handed gloves given to him by his sympathetic men.

If a soldier became sick, or was hurt in battle, he was in serious trouble. In the 1860s, there were no medicines to fight infections. The powerful bullets fired by Civil War rifles often smashed the arm or leg bones of gunshot victims. Doctors could not repair bone injuries, so they usually cut off a damaged limb to save the patient. The only painkillers available for this surgery were chloroform, ether, or whiskey. But more soldiers were killed by camp illnesses than by battle wounds. Polluted drinking water gave troops diphtheria and cholera. Tens of thousands of men died of these diseases as well as of measles, mumps, malaria, and yellow fever. Cures for these illnesses would not be discovered until several decades later.

Medical uniform
This is the homespun "butternut" uniform of Confederate Major William H. Harrison. He provided the South's Army of Tennessee with medical supplies. Union army medical officers' uniforms were distinguished by black stripes down the outside pants seams.

Part-time ambulance workers
In both armies, cooks and musicians worked as stretcher bearers during battles. This photograph shows Union Zouave troops performing an ambulance drill.

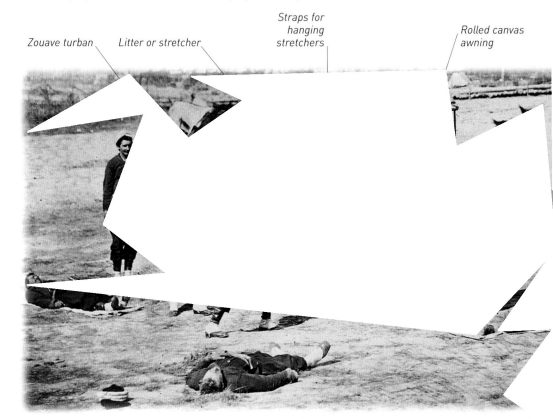

Zouave turban   Litter or stretcher   Straps for hanging stretchers   Rolled canvas awning

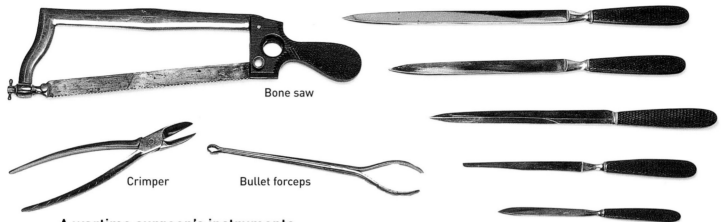

Bone saw

Crimper

Bullet forceps

Amputation knives

A wartime surgeon's instruments

A bullet forceps, used to extract bullets, a crimper for snipping off bits of shattered bone, and a bone saw were the tools surgeons used most after battles. Many soldiers had to have shattered limbs amputated during the war.

Temporary graves

Because the railroads were busy, the bodies of those who died during the war were not always sent home for burial immediately. This photograph shows temporary graves outside a Union army hospital. When the war ended, many of these bodies were shipped home for final burial.

ARMY OF THE CONFEDERATE STATES.

CERTIFICATE OF DISABILITY FOR DISCHARGE.

An honorable discharge

When a soldier was too sick or hurt to continue in the army, a doctor gave him a certificate of disability. This form prevented the disabled man from being drafted back into service.

Zouave drum

A right-armed general ...

Union General Philip Kearny (right) had lost his left arm in combat before the Civil War. He was one of many officers who continued to serve even though they had lost an arm, a leg, or an eye.

One white dress glove

French-style kepi

... And a left-armed general

Union General Oliver Howard lost his right arm in action. General Kearny, missing his left arm, visited Howard in the hospital and joked that now they could buy gloves together. Howard continued to soldier on through the war with only one arm.

Confederate general's stars

Joseph E. Johnston
Johnston was a US Army brigadier general who joined Southern service to lead Jefferson Davis's troops in Virginia.

Great commanders

Some of the best-known soldiers and sailors in US history earned their reputations in the Civil War. Philip Sheridan, a Union cavalry general, became known for several Civil War victories. Many Southern commanders, such as Robert E. Lee and Joseph E. Johnston, gave up powerful positions in the US armed forces to serve the Confederacy. Others found opportunity. General Ulysses S. Grant was a poor store clerk before the war. The conflict gave him a chance to show he could be a leader.

Grant's war horse Cincinnati

Lieutenant general's stars

Ulysses S. Grant
Before the war, Ulysses S. Grant considered himself a failure. However, he achieved early success in the war and gained promotion for his victory at the Battle of Shiloh in Tennessee, 1862. He later became general-in-chief of all Union armies and defeated Robert E. Lee's army in April, 1865. His fame helped to win him the US presidency in 1868.

Stonewall Jackson
Southern general Thomas Jackson was a professor at the Virginia Military Institute when the Civil War began. He won his nickname, Stonewall, for his tough action at the First Battle of Bull Run. In May, 1863, he was wounded in the Battle of Chancellorsville, Virginia, and died several days later.

George B. McClellan
George B. McClellan led the Union's Army of the Potomac in the Battle of Antietam, Maryland, in September 1862. After that inconclusive fight, he was fired by President Lincoln. After the war, he became governor of New Jersey.

Robert E. Lee

Robert E. Lee was the son of Revolutionary War hero Harry Lee. Nationally known for his 1859 capture of abolitionist fanatic John Brown, he turned down an offer to lead the Union's largest army in 1861, and instead remained loyal to his home state of Virginia.

W. T. Sherman

William T. Sherman had been an army officer before the war. From the Battle of Shiloh onward, he became a friend of U. S. Grant. He is remembered for burning Atlanta and for devastating the state of Georgia on a campaign called the March to the Sea.

Sherman's war horse Lexington

J. E. B. Stuart

James Ewell Brown Stuart led Robert E. Lee's cavalry corps until mortally wounded at the Battle of Yellow Tavern, Virginia, in 1864. He was famous for taking chances.

Raphael Semmes

Confederate Admiral Raphael Semmes, nicknamed "Pirate" Semmes, commanded vessels that attacked Union merchant ships around the globe. This challenged the rules of warfare and made Semmes famous.

Admiral's rank insignia

Cuff braid indicating rank

Philip Sheridan

Sheridan was the Union's most successful cavalry commander. He led Civil War infantry, then commanded the army's cavalry in Virginia. As a cavalry leader, he helped defeat Robert E. Lee at Appomattox.

Admiral David Farragut

David Farragut is the naval commander who said, "Damn the torpedoes! Full speed ahead!" He won the surrender of New Orleans in 1862 and made his famous statement while winning the Battle of Mobile Bay in 1864.

Arming soldiers

Early volunteers carried a variety of weapons. The rifles they preferred were single-shot guns loaded at the muzzle—the firing end of the rifle. To load the rifle, a soldier first poured gunpowder down the muzzle. Next, he placed the bullet in the muzzle and rammed it down the barrel with a metal rod called a ramrod. To fire the rifle, he placed a metal cap filled with explosive on a metal piece called a nipple. When he cocked back the rifle's hammer and pulled its trigger, the hammer hit the cap and fired the weapon.

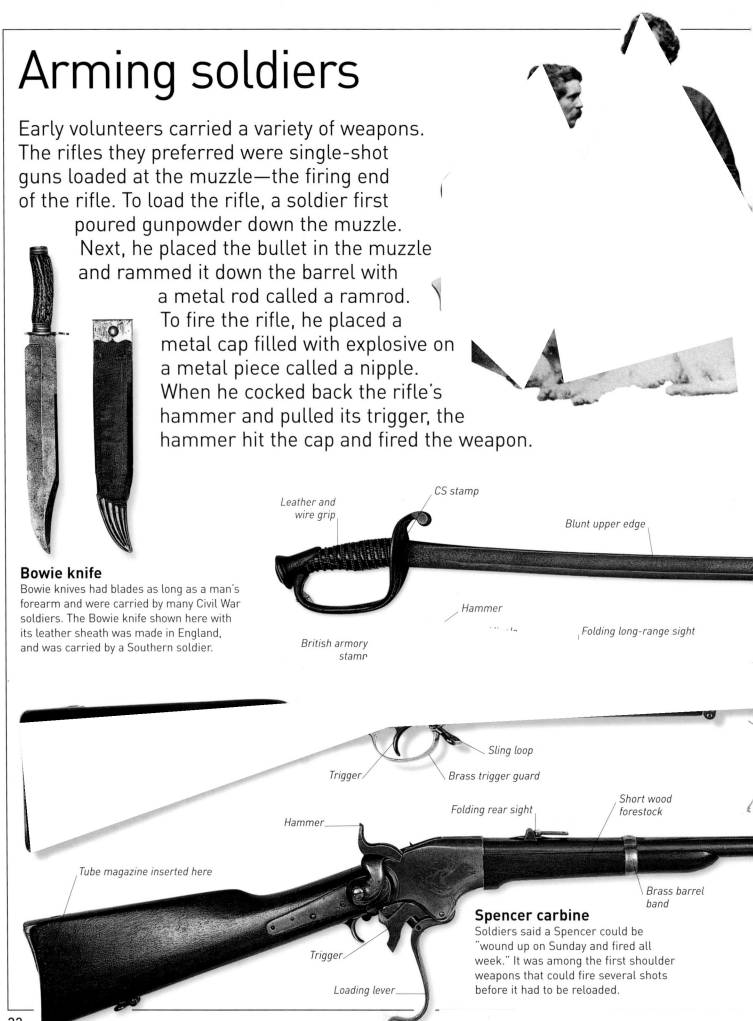

Bowie knife

Bowie knives had blades as long as a man's forearm and were carried by many Civil War soldiers. The Bowie knife shown here with its leather sheath was made in England, and was carried by a Southern soldier.

Leather and wire grip

CS stamp

Blunt upper edge

Hammer

Folding long-range sight

British armory stamp

Sling loop

Trigger

Brass trigger guard

Folding rear sight

Short wood forestock

Hammer

Tube magazine inserted here

Brass barrel band

Spencer carbine

Soldiers said a Spencer could be "wound up on Sunday and fired all week." It was among the first shoulder weapons that could fire several shots before it had to be reloaded.

Trigger

Loading lever

32

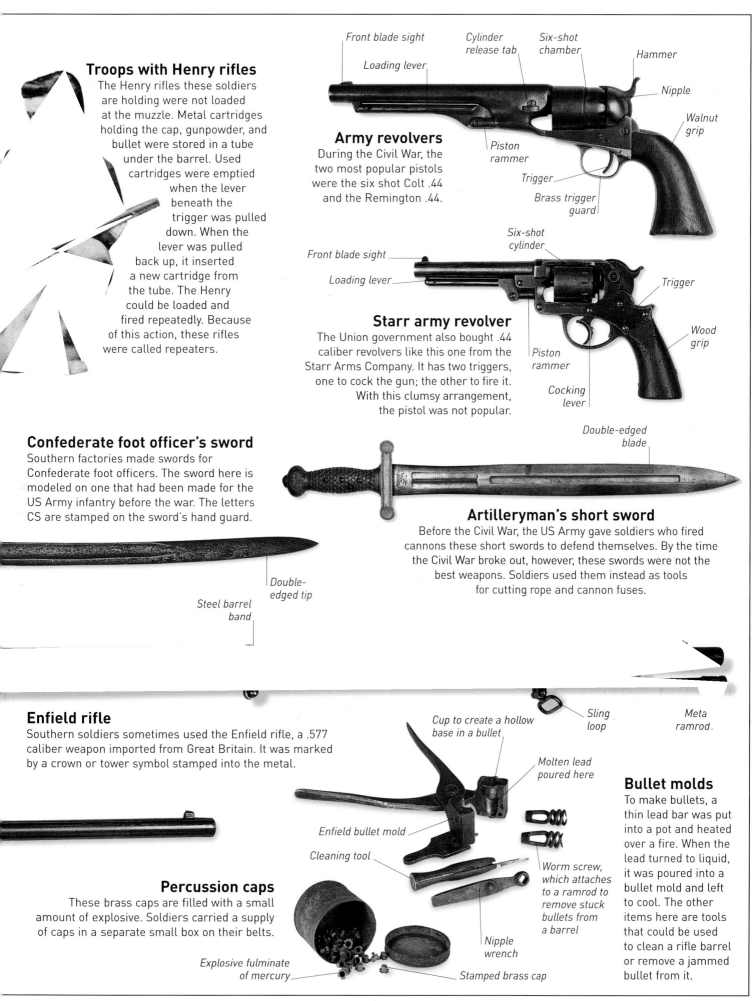

Troops with Henry rifles

The Henry rifles these soldiers are holding were not loaded at the muzzle. Metal cartridges holding the cap, gunpowder, and bullet were stored in a tube under the barrel. Used cartridges were emptied when the lever beneath the trigger was pulled down. When the lever was pulled back up, it inserted a new cartridge from the tube. The Henry could be loaded and fired repeatedly. Because of this action, these rifles were called repeaters.

Front blade sight
Loading lever
Cylinder release tab
Six-shot chamber
Hammer
Nipple
Walnut grip
Piston rammer
Trigger
Brass trigger guard

Army revolvers

During the Civil War, the two most popular pistols were the six shot Colt .44 and the Remington .44.

Front blade sight
Loading lever
Six-shot cylinder
Trigger
Wood grip
Piston rammer
Cocking lever

Starr army revolver

The Union government also bought .44 caliber revolvers like this one from the Starr Arms Company. It has two triggers, one to cock the gun; the other to fire it. With this clumsy arrangement, the pistol was not popular.

Confederate foot officer's sword

Southern factories made swords for Confederate foot officers. The sword here is modeled on one that had been made for the US Army infantry before the war. The letters CS are stamped on the sword's hand guard.

Double-edged blade

Artilleryman's short sword

Before the Civil War, the US Army gave soldiers who fired cannons these short swords to defend themselves. By the time the Civil War broke out, however, these swords were not the best weapons. Soldiers used them instead as tools for cutting rope and cannon fuses.

Double-edged tip
Steel barrel band

Enfield rifle

Southern soldiers sometimes used the Enfield rifle, a .577 caliber weapon imported from Great Britain. It was marked by a crown or tower symbol stamped into the metal.

Cup to create a hollow base in a bullet
Sling loop
Meta ramrod
Molten lead poured here
Enfield bullet mold
Cleaning tool
Worm screw, which attaches to a ramrod to remove stuck bullets from a barrel

Bullet molds

To make bullets, a thin lead bar was put into a pot and heated over a fire. When the lead turned to liquid, it was poured into a bullet mold and left to cool. The other items here are tools that could be used to clean a rifle barrel or remove a jammed bullet from it.

Percussion caps

These brass caps are filled with a small amount of explosive. Soldiers carried a supply of caps in a separate small box on their belts.

Nipple wrench
Explosive fulminate of mercury
Stamped brass cap

Black volunteers

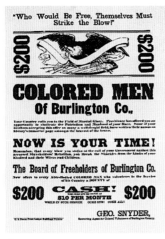

A call to arms
Many Northern communities wanted to raise units of black volunteers. Posters were displayed throughout counties to recruit black troops.

In 1860, there were fewer than 500,000 "free Negroes" in the US. Almost four million blacks were held in slavery. When the war started, free blacks could not join the Union army. In 1863, Lincoln issued the Emancipation Proclamation, stating that all slaves living in Confederate states were to be considered free. Congress then passed a law allowing black men to join the Union army. They were paid less than white soldiers, and if they were captured, they were shot or enslaved. However, these risks did not stop black men from taking part in combat. Several black soldiers won the Union's highest award for bravery, the Medal of Honor.

Fighting men
Some prejudiced Northerners believed that black volunteers should do heavy labor and small tasks in the army, rather than fight. When given the chance, though, black soldiers proved their bravery in combat.

Flags for a black regiment
Black regiments were called US Colored Troops, or U.S.C.T. for short. Here, the men of the 20th U.S.C.T. are given flags to carry off to war in front of a cheering New York City crowd in 1864.

A slave hero
Robert Smalls was a slave in Charleston, South Carolina. One day he hijacked a ship loaded with new Confederate cannons. His wife and children were also onboard. Smalls turned the Southern ship and its cargo over to the Union navy. He was rewarded and his family was freed from slavery. After the war, he was elected to the US House of Representatives.

A rejected volunteer
Attitudes about race were not the same all over the South. In 1812, free black volunteers had fought to defend New Orleans in Louisiana. When the Civil War broke out, free blacks raised the Louisiana Native Guards regiment to defend New Orleans once again. But the Confederate government could not overcome its racial prejudice and would not allow the Native Guards into its army.

Canvas four-man tent

Main camp

Mattross, a wood piece used to move a carriage tail

Rammer

Proud black cannoneers

Not long before posing with their cannon, these black artillerymen were slaves. They were among thousands of escaped slaves who were organized into army regiments late in the war. Many of them became crack soldiers.

Colonel Robert Gould Shaw

The bravest black regiment

In 1863, Massachusetts governor John Andrew selected Robert Gould Shaw, the son of a prominent white family of abolitionists, to lead an all-black regiment. In July 1863, the regiment, named the 54th Massachusetts, was asked to charge heavily armed Confederates at Fort Wagner, outside Charleston, South Carolina. Colonel Shaw was the first to reach the top of the fort. He was killed there as he shouted, "Onward, Fifty-fourth!" The attack failed and cost the regiment 272 troopers.

Slave to soldier

This photograph of a young black Union army drummer named Jackson was circulated across the North, together with a photograph of the same boy dressed in the rags he had been wearing when he arrived as an escaped slave. The photographs were shown to convince Northern doubters that slaves could be trained to fight for the freedom of others.

The horsemen

The American Civil War was the last large conflict in history in which soldiers on horseback played an important part. Cavalrymen scouted out the positions of enemy armies and made shock attacks to break up infantry formations. If an enemy army retreated, cavalry troops were expected to pursue it. Additionally, horse soldiers were used as messengers and as armed escorts for prisoners. Within decades, these cavalry jobs were replaced by telephones, automobiles, tanks, and biplanes. But in the 1860s, horse soldiers saw themselves as mounted knights.

Colt revolver

18-gauge shotgun barrel

LeMat revolver

Cavalry revolvers and holster
The .44 caliber Colt revolver was a popular Civil War cavalry weapon. It was carried in a leather holster, like the one shown here, on the left side of a trooper's belt. The LeMat revolver fired nine .40 caliber slugs. It also featured a short second barrel that fired an 18-gauge shotgun round.

Horse soldier
Soldiers often tried to look warlike in photographs. The Mississippi trooper in this image is holding one of his cavalry weapons, a six-shot black powder revolver.

Bit

Halter

Reins

Sabers of the North and South
The US Army Model 1850 saber was carried by both Northern and Southern troopers during the Civil War. Confederate factories produced thousands of copies of it for Southern horsemen to carry into battle.

Leather and wire grip

Hilt

Model 1850 saber

Hilt hook to catch and turn away an enemy blade

Sharpened upper edge

Confederate saber

Pommel   *Hand guard*   *Hammer*   *Steel breech holds a single shot.*   *Front blade sight*

Walnut stock

Wood forestock   *Steel barrel*

Trigger

Steel trigger guard and loading lever, which pulls down to open the breech

A Sharps carbine
The .52 caliber Sharps carbine was a single-shot weapon. Its trigger guard was also a loading lever. When pulled down, the lever opened a slot near the hammer, where the cartridge was inserted. This allowed soldiers to load and fire it about eight times a minute.

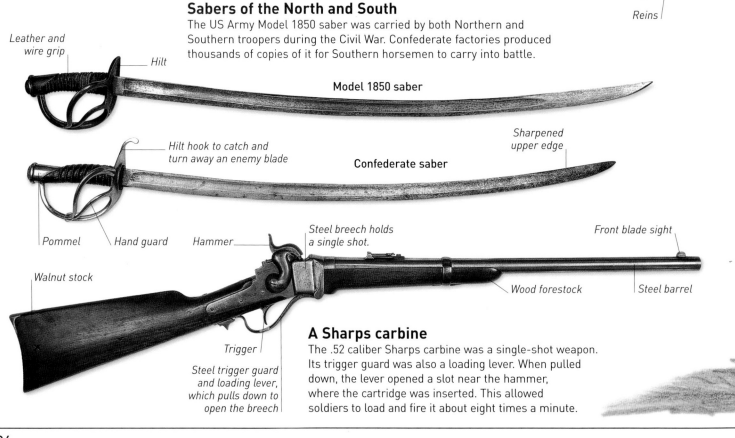

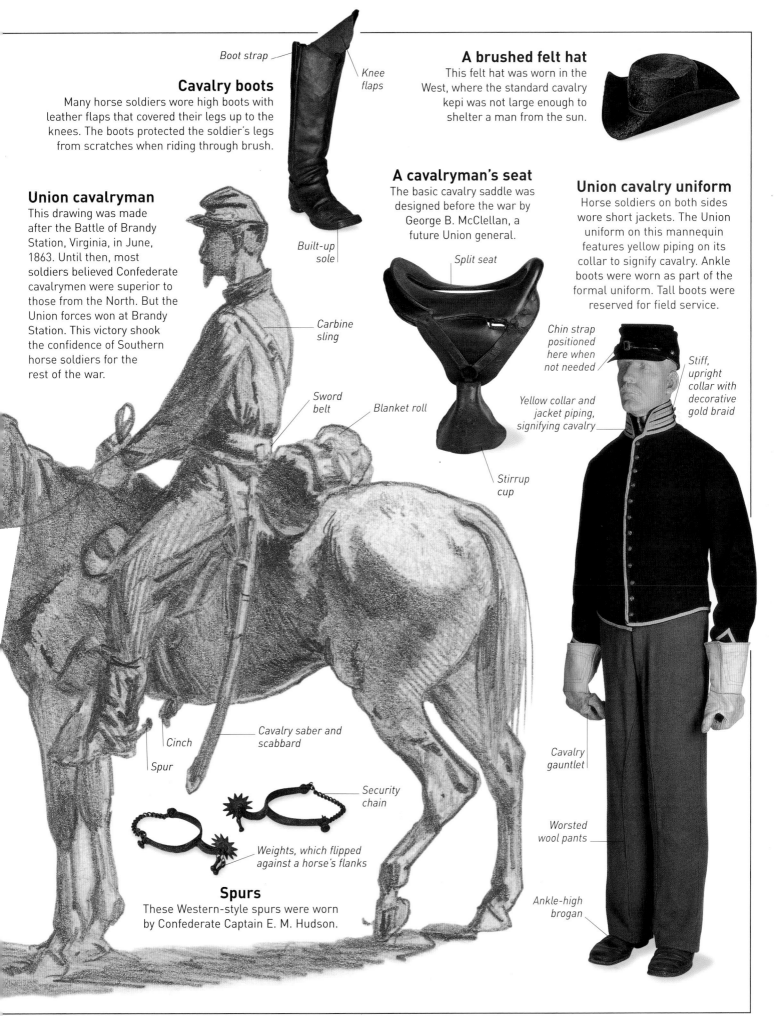

Cavalry boots

Many horse soldiers wore high boots with leather flaps that covered their legs up to the knees. The boots protected the soldier's legs from scratches when riding through brush.

Boot strap

Knee flaps

Built-up sole

A brushed felt hat

This felt hat was worn in the West, where the standard cavalry kepi was not large enough to shelter a man from the sun.

Union cavalryman

This drawing was made after the Battle of Brandy Station, Virginia, in June, 1863. Until then, most soldiers believed Confederate cavalrymen were superior to those from the North. But the Union forces won at Brandy Station. This victory shook the confidence of Southern horse soldiers for the rest of the war.

A cavalryman's seat

The basic cavalry saddle was designed before the war by George B. McClellan, a future Union general.

Split seat

Stirrup cup

Union cavalry uniform

Horse soldiers on both sides wore short jackets. The Union uniform on this mannequin features yellow piping on its collar to signify cavalry. Ankle boots were worn as part of the formal uniform. Tall boots were reserved for field service.

Carbine sling

Sword belt

Blanket roll

Chin strap positioned here when not needed

Yellow collar and jacket piping, signifying cavalry

Stiff, upright collar with decorative gold braid

Cinch

Spur

Cavalry saber and scabbard

Security chain

Weights, which flipped against a horse's flanks

Cavalry gauntlet

Worsted wool pants

Ankle-high brogan

Spurs

These Western-style spurs were worn by Confederate Captain E. M. Hudson.

Army camp life

Soldiers spent almost all their time outdoors. On campaigns, most men slept on the ground, wrapped in blankets. In the cities, troops often lived in simple wood buildings called barracks. But when assigned to large camps, the troops slept in tents that held up to eight men. Their meals were cooked on portable ovens in large tent kitchens. Soldiers spent their days practicing drills, repairing equipment, and doing chores. In their free time, they wrote letters, read, gambled, or enjoyed concerts put on by their unit's marching bands.

Outside the barracks
This 1861 photograph shows Union troops at their barracks. Signs on the wall indicate the men belong to their regiment's Company I. The soldiers in front are playing cards with the company drummer.

Bass saxhorn

Musician's sword

Playing cards
Card playing was popular in the camps. But many soldiers would throw away their cards before going into battle. If they were killed, they did not want their relatives to know they had been gambling.

Set for dinner
Troops used tin plates and drank from tin cups. They ate with a unique folding fork, spoon, and knife combination, which took up little room in the knapsack.

Hardtack was a staple ration for the Civil War soldiers

Tin plate

PARADE
POLKA MARCH.
AS PLAYED BY THE
N. O. Washington Artillery Band.

Making music
These members of a Union Army marching band are holding a saxhorn, an instrument that is no longer played. The cover sheet is for a lively military number made popular by the Confederate Army's Washington Artillery Band of New Orleans.

Combination fork, spoon, knife

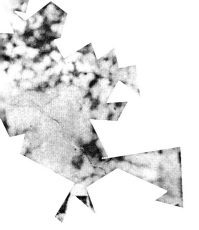

Winter's cold
A Confederate soldier painted this scene of his "winter quarters." In winter, troops built crude wood cabins to stave off the cold.

Photographs
During the Civil War, soldiers often carried photographs of their loved ones with them. This photograph of a Southern soldier's little girl was carried in a hinged, leather case.

Writing home
A letter was the quickest way for a soldier to get a message home. Telegraphic messages were expensive and were controlled by the military. These are some writing implements of a Union soldier, as well as a letter and a rolled-up lap desk. When unrolled, the desk provided a smooth writing surface for a soldier seated on the ground.

Wood slats covered with cloth

Machine-made paper

Opening slides over barrel

Three-sided spike

Postmark

Envelope with patriotic illustrations

Pen nibs

Useful weapon
This is a steel parade model of the most common bayonet used in the Civil War. Most were made of iron. The bayonets were sometimes used as tent pegs or candlesticks. In a crisis, bayonets also served as handy digging tools.

Field artillery

Cannons were the deadliest weapons in the Civil War. Some had barrels cut with grooves to help the cannonballs fly on long, straight paths. But most were smoothbores with no grooves. To load the cannon, a bag of gunpowder was pushed down the barrel with a pole. Then the cannonball was placed in the barrel. A crew member made a hole in the gunpowder bag with a long, wire needle called a pick. Next a fuse was placed into the hole at the barrel's base, and a long string was attached to a pin set into the top of the fuse. When the string was pulled, the pin popped out of the fuse, causing a spark to shoot down the barrel. At that point, the gunpowder exploded and sent the cannonball shooting out of the gun's mouth.

Telescope

Traveling through mud

At the time of the Civil War, there were few paved roads. In wet weather, thousands of marching soldiers and horses turned routes into muddy bogs. Troops often had to help their huge horses pull heavy guns through the muck to reach the battlefield.

Brass pendulum

This pendulum device was set at the base of the barrel to show whether the gun was level.

Elevation gauge

Blade sight

Pendulum weight

Gun sight

To aim a gun, a crewman set a portable sight on the base and lined it up with a simple blade sight that screwed into a spot on top of the muzzle.

Prolonge, a thick rope

Bubble level

Hitch

Carriage tail

Moving guns across the water

Moving cannons across a river was difficult. If there was time, the guns were taken apart and floated across on small boats. When the army was in a hurry, fully assembled cannons were floated on vessels wrapped in waterproof blankets.

"Napoleon"

The most common cannon was the Model 1857 gun-howitzer. Soldiers called this smoothbore bronze gun a Napoleon. It was named after Louis-Napoléon, the emperor of France at the time.

Iron shot

Case shot

This iron shot, known as case shot, was filled with slugs and gunpowder. A time fuse was screwed into the opening. When fired, the case shot would explode in midair, raining bullets over the enemy.

Fuse hole

Lead balls

As attacking troops raced toward an army's guns, artillerymen fired canister rounds at them. These were thin tin cans filled with lead balls and sawdust. They came apart at the cannon's mouth and sprayed deadly lead slugs at the enemy.

Lead slugs

Solid iron ball

Strapping

Sabot

Thumb stall

Before a cannon was reloaded, it had to be sponged out. A crew member held his thumb over the hot fuse hole to cut off the air supply to any burning debris. This leather cover protected his thumb from the heat.

Sabot

Cannonballs were strapped to a round piece of wood called a sabot, which kept the balls from rolling around in the ammunition chest and allowed them to sit well on top of a gunpowder bag inside the barrel.

Quarter-second marks

Explosion timer

A pewter cap was screwed into case shot rounds. Gunners punched a hole in the fuse face on the spot that indicated the number of seconds they wanted the fuse to burn.

Cast-bronze tube

Leather vent cover to keep rainwater out of the tube

Detachable blade sight

Cascabel, used to maneuver the gun

Swab

Prolonge hook

Sponge

Spoke

Rammer

Iron wheel band

Hub

Wood wheel rim

Gettysburg

Gettysburg is a small town in Pennsylvania, just north of the Maryland state line. In the summer of 1863, Confederate General Robert E. Lee marched 75,000 men north to invade Union territory. On July 1, a small Union force met and fought them there until reinforcements arrived. The Union leader, General George Meade, had an army of more than 88,000 men. The next day, the troops fought over important spots bordering the town. On the morning of July 3, there was a fight around Culp's Hill. Then Lee told a division led by Major General George Pickett to attack Meade's battle line. Thousands of Confederates ran directly at Union cannons and riflemen. A huge number of Southerners were killed and wounded during "Pickett's Charge." This defeat forced Lee to retreat south on July 4. His fight with Meade was the largest battle ever fought in North America.

George Meade
President Lincoln made George Meade commander of the Union's Army of the Potomac just two days before Gettysburg. Meade replaced General Joseph Hooker, who was defeated in May 1863, at the Battle of Chancellorsville, Virginia.

Gunner ramming in a canister round

Drum modeled on the instrument shown on the opposite page

Little Round Top

Dusk attack
At dusk on July 2, two Confederate brigades from General Early's division rushed Union troops at the gatehouse of Gettysburg's cemetery. Union reinforcements pushed them back, with many casualties. Newspaper artist Arthur Berghaus sketched the attack.

Harry Hays
Confederate General Harry Hays led troops in the failed dusk attack on Union troops at the cemetery. He was defeated, but survived the battle. After the war, he served as sheriff of New Orleans.

Pickett's Charge
Southerners in Pickett's Charge actually reached the Union battle lines. This painting shows Confederate General Lewis Armistead with his upraised sword beside a Union cannon. He was mortally wounded on the spot.

Battle honors

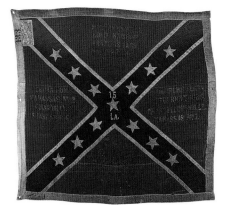

When a regiment served honorably in a battle, it was permitted to stitch the name of that fight onto its battle flag. Here is the flag of the 15th Louisiana Regiment. The Gettysburg battle honor is stitched just below the center of the blue Saint Andrew's cross.

Gettysburg dead

Photographers arrived at Gettysburg immediately after the battle. This photograph shows the bodies of some of the soldiers from Georgia and South Carolina.

Main Union line in the valley below

Little Round Top

This hill gave soldiers a good view of the battlefield. Both armies knew they had to seize it to win. Southern troops charged it but were defeated by the 20th Maine Regiment. The Maine troops ran out of bullets, but they surprised the Southerners with a bayonet charge.

Animal hide drum head

A battle drum

This drum, found on the battlefield, was used as a model for a drum in Peter Rothermel's famous painting of the fight. Drummers beat out signals that directed the troops to move one way or another.

Strapping to keep the drum head taut

Hand-painted eagle and crest

Trees marking the center of Meade's lines   *General Lewis Armistead*

Vicksburg

Vicksburg, Mississippi, is a town on the east bank of the Mississippi River between Memphis, Tennessee, and New Orleans, Louisiana. The Confederate army greatly fortified Vicksburg and set up cannons that could fire on any ships passing by. In late 1862 and early 1863, Union commander Ulysses S. Grant sent several Northern forces to Vicksburg. Each campaign failed. Then in May, 1863, Grant maneuvered an army behind the town. After some small battles, he drove Vicksburg's defenders inside the town's fortifications. Meanwhile, the Union navy began shelling the town from the river. Grant's forces surrounded Vicksburg for more than 40 days. No food or ammunition entered it. After more than a month of hunger and repeated shelling, Confederate General John Pemberton surrendered on July 4.

Civilian bomb shelters
Some Vicksburg citizens lived in what they called "dugouts" or "bomb proofs." As this photograph shows, these were simply holes dug into the town's hillsides.

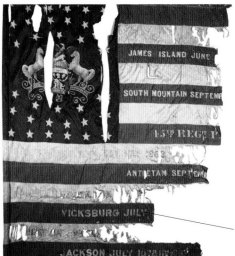

Honors
Regiments that served at Vicksburg were allowed to add the town's name to their list of battle honors. Here the flag of the 51st Pennsylvania shows Vicksburg among the battle names on its tattered banner.

Battle honor

Canopies
The summer sun in Mississippi is fierce. Many Northern troops at Vicksburg came from cool-weather states such as Minnesota and Wisconsin. As this newspaper drawing shows, the soldiers put canopies over their trenches to ward off sunstroke and dehydration.

Vicksburg leader
Confederate General John C. Pemberton led the failed defense of Vicksburg. When angry Southerners were blaming him for the loss, many of them pointed out that John Pemberton was a native of Pennsylvania. He had married a Southern woman and thrown his loyalty behind her family and her part of the country when the war came.

Shells

Union artillerymen brought heavy rifled cannons to Vicksburg. This assortment of shells shows the grooves or fins that allowed these rounds to travel in a straight path to their targets over long distances.

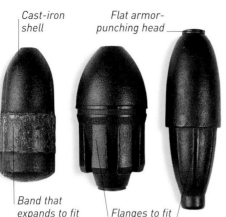

Cast-iron shell

Flat armor-punching head

Band that expands to fit the gun's rifling

Flanges to fit the rifling

Victors marching into town

On July 4, 1863, Grant's troops marched into Vicksburg. This newspaper illustration shows the US flag flying over the Vicksburg courthouse. This Union victory came one day after the Northern army's other success at Gettysburg in Pennsylvania.

Attacking trenches

Early in the siege, Union soldiers rushed the Confederate trenches several times. Some were shot down as they tried to scale ditches. Others were killed as they ran across open ground. After these assaults failed, Union cannons began firing on the town nonstop.

Stiff paper to stabilize fins

Steel grenade jacket

Lightweight wood stem

Detonation plunger plate exploded the grenade.

A hand grenade

Northerners sometimes used Ketchum hand grenades that exploded when they landed on the detonation plates. Confederates tried to catch these grenades in blankets, then threw them back at the attacking Union troops.

Northern life

Citizens of New England and the Midwest were stunned when the Southern states left the Union. When the Confederates fired on Fort Sumter, that shock turned to anger. Many volunteered immediately to fight for the Union. But until July, 1863, Union armies often lost on the battlefield. Through that period, the North's real success was on the home front. Industries in Northern towns took on extra men and, in some places, even employed women. After President Lincoln signed the Homestead Act of 1862, many immigrants headed west to make new homes on free frontier land. While Southerners were suffering food and clothing shortages, and their rebellious nation was shrinking in size daily, the Union was growing larger and richer.

A tragic First Lady
Mary Todd Lincoln was from a Kentucky slave-holding family and had relatives who served in the Confederate military. She married Abraham Lincoln in 1842. Sadly, two of their four sons died before Lincoln's assassination in 1865, and a third son died in 1871. Subsequently, Mrs. Lincoln suffered a series of emotional illnesses and was cared for by her eldest son, Robert Lincoln. She died in 1882.

A JOB FOR THE NEW CABINETMAKER.
From *Frank Leslie's Illustrated Newspaper*, February 2, 1861.

Wool tray

A wishful cartoon
President Lincoln was often teased in political cartoons. But sometimes he was praised. This cartoon, published shortly after his 1860 election victory, expressed the public's hope that the new leader could bring the nation back together.

A tool of Union victory
Many historians claim Northern industry won the war for the Union. This wool-carding machine from a factory in Pennsylvania made wool that could be turned into military uniforms. The South supplied manufacturers with raw materials, such as cotton, but it lacked large amounts of machinery and workers to make products for its own use.

A machine of progress
Called a universal driver, this steam engine could be attached to many different manufacturing devices. Its boiler was fed by coal, a raw material that the North had in abundance.

Steam supply from boiler • Gear lever • Driving wheel

Pistons • Driving rod • Cam

Baseball
Organized baseball gathered a foothold during the Civil War years. Northern towns had the peace, prosperity, and leisure time to establish simple baseball leagues. This is an 1864 photograph of the Brooklyn Atlantics baseball team. The Atlantics had their team photographs mounted on cardboard. The photographs were passed around like modern-day baseball cards.

Carding roll

Drive gear

Belt drive wheel

Confederate culture

The Confederate States of America existed for four years, from the spring of 1861 to the spring of 1865. During those years, this rebel nation chose a president and a vice president, elected members to a House of Representatives and a Senate, and set up a Supreme Court. The Confederacy also printed its own currency, raised a national flag, and adopted a constitution identical to that of the United States—except that the Confederate constitution contained an amendment guaranteeing the existence of slavery.

Southern press
The *Southern Illustrated News* was one of the few publications read throughout the South. It was modeled on Northern newspapers such as *Harper's Weekly*.

Jefferson and Varina Davis
Jefferson Davis (left) was the only president the Southern nation ever had. He was elected to a six-year term. As a young man, he married the daughter of future US President Zachary Taylor. His bride died just months after their wedding. His second wife, Varina Howell Davis (right) was the First Lady of the Confederate States of America and mother of their six children. Following her husband's death in 1889, she moved to New York City and supported herself as a professional writer.

Upright collar

Satin vest lapel

Copy of an official portrait of Varina Davis

Fan

Cameo bracelet

At play during the war
Southerners tried to amuse themselves during the war years with games, books, and theater. These Confederate women are escaping their worries by playing a game of croquet.

Worthless money
At the start of the war, the Confederate government backed up its paper currency with gold and the cotton industry. Over time, however, much of the gold was spent, and it became hard to ship cotton abroad. Soon, items that had sold for $2 in the South cost $20. Confederate currency gradually became worth less and less as the war continued.

War substitutes

This is the dress coat of Confederate General D. W. Adams. Regulations called for his uniform to be made of gray wool, but this coat is made of denim. In the war's last days, most Southerners wore and ate things made of substitute items because they could not obtain raw materials. Coffee, for example, was made from chicory and flour was made from ground acorns.

Southern industry

This photograph is of a gunpowder factory in Augusta, Georgia. To manufacture explosives, the factory needed a material called niter. This ingredient could not be obtained in quantity from Southern mines. Instead, factory chemists got niter by processing the contents of chamber pots they had collected throughout the county.

A Southern aristocrat

Caroline Deslonde was the daughter of a plantation owner in Louisiana. Shortly before the war, she married Pierre Beauregard, one of the Confederacy's first hero-generals. Caroline was a member of the wealthy class of Southerners who had a strong influence on politics and society. Many poorer Southerners blamed these people for the war and its hardships.

President
Jefferson Davis

Vice President
Alexander Stephens

Mrs. Lucy Pickens,
First Lady of
South Carolina

Secretary of
War George
W. Randolph

General Thomas
"Stonewall" Jackson

War on the water

The navies of the North and South played an important role in the war. Union sailors fought Confederates on the rivers and blocked Southern seaports. President Davis's navy commissioned vessels that attacked Union merchant ships and stole their cargoes. The navies also changed the technology of warfare. The South produced the world's first ironclad warship, the CSS *Virginia*. In return, the Union built an ironclad named the *Monitor*. To defend against Union vessels, Confederate engineers perfected floating explosive mines that threatened ships entering Southern waters.

Iron armor
Iron armor was no guarantee of safety. This newspaper drawing shows how the blast of one ironclad ship's guns rocks the other. Shells fired at close range tore at the iron and splintered the metal plates' wood backing. Flying shards of metal and wood often killed or wounded the sailors inside.

Lock plate

Hammer

Trigger guard

Trigger

Edged upper tip

Sling loop

Wood stock

Jenks carbine
Sailors were often given short-barreled rifles to defend themselves because these weapons were easier to load in the cramped conditions of a ship. This rifle is a powerful .54 caliber Jenks carbine.

The Alabama *seized 64 Union merchant ships with cargoes valued at more than $6.5 million*

The *Alabama*
Commanded by Admiral Semmes, the Confederate raider *Alabama* was built secretly in the UK and had a crew of foreign volunteers. It attacked Union merchant ships in the Atlantic and stalked the waters around Africa and the Mediterranean.

A spyglass
The telescope allowed crews to observe enemy ships or survey a coastline from a safe distance. This Civil War spyglass is US Navy issue.

A semisubmersible
The Confederate vessel in this photograph is called a David. This class of vessel was semisubmersible. This means it settled low in the water so that only its top was visible. It carried an explosive device attached to a wood beam. The beam jutted from the David's nose and was rammed into the side of an enemy ship. These vessels usually operated at night.

Folding smokestack

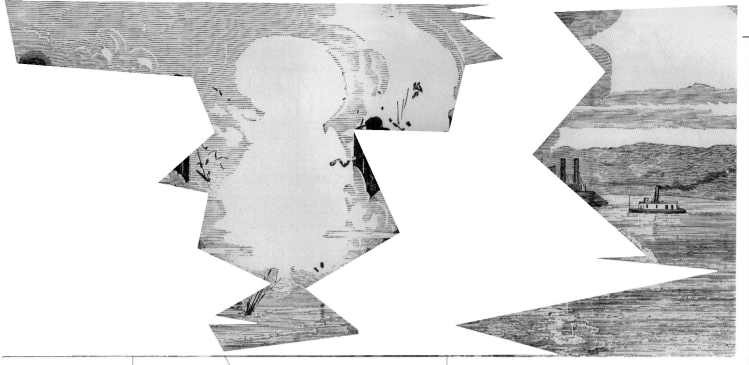

Iron plates, held on with rivets

Brass barrel band

Armored paddlewheel cover

Sloping iron sides to deflect cannonballs

Wood forestock

Steel blade

Grip

Brass hand guard

A Union navy cutlass
Although they carried rifles and revolvers, Civil War sailors still relied on "cold steel" in a fight. This Union navy cutlass was one of dozens of blades stored on the ship's main deck.

CSS *Arkansas*
This 10-gun Confederate vessel was armored with railroad rails and iron plates. As a Union fleet approached it in Louisiana, in August, 1862, its engines broke down. To keep it out of Union hands, the crew set it on fire and abandoned it. The *Arkansas* floated downriver and sank.

Mines
This drawing shows how wooden mines were floated just below the surface of the water. Many nations believed that the use of submerged mines was cowardly and a breach of the rules of warfare.

A Union minesweeper
This is the Union ironclad *Saugus* on Virginia's James River. A brave Union naval officer stands on a platform above a net that juts from its prow. He directs the ironclad to sweep up an explosive mine. If the device explodes, the officer could be killed.

A nineteenth-century mine
Wooden or tin containers of explosives were placed in harbors and rivers. Called torpedoes or mines, some of them were fitted with detonators. If a passing ship struck one of the mines, it exploded and sank the vessel. This mine is made of wood.

The secret war

During the Civil War, groups of civilians called guerrillas often banded together to attack enemy troops. Confederate attorney John Mosby organized a group called the Partisan Rangers to operate in Virginia's Blue Ridge Mountain region. At night they rode behind enemy lines to attack and capture Union troops. Spies were another danger, reporting military plans and movements to the enemy. This secret warfare is called espionage. Elizabeth Van Lew of Richmond, Virginia, was a mature, single woman who held strong pro-Union opinions, but was a member of a wealthy family living in the Confederate capital. Van Lew pretended to suffer from mild mental illness. Southern government leaders often spoke freely in her presence, believing she was harmless. Using couriers, Van Lew sent word of what she heard to Union military leaders.

A hanged spy
Confederate spy Lawrence Williams was a cousin of Mrs. Robert E. Lee. He was caught wearing a US Army uniform, claiming to be a member of the inspector general's staff. He was questioned, then hanged.

A successful spy
Henry Thomas Harrison (above) was a Confederate army officer who worked as a spy. He pinpointed Union army positions during General Lee's invasion of the North in 1863, bringing on the Battle of Gettysburg. Here he holds a coded message that reads "I love you."

The gray ghost
Armed with up to eight revolvers, John Mosby rode out at night in a feathered hat and cape to gather his guerrilla band. His men attacked Union troops, supply depots, and camps. In the South, he was a hero—always escaping capture. To Union troops, he was the "Gray Ghost," a danger of the night.

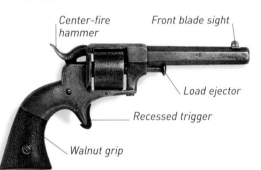

Center-fire hammer · Front blade sight · Load ejector · Recessed trigger · Walnut grip

Rejected by soldiers but not by spies
Secret volunteers used any weapon they could find to carry on their underground war. Many of their arms were military rejects. This Allen & Wheelock center-fire pistol was manufactured as a .44 caliber "Army" revolver, but it was never widely used by the military.

A detective spy
At the start of the Civil War, Allen Pinkerton was a successful private detective. Union General George McClellan hired him to organize a body of spies for his army. But Pinkerton was not good at espionage. He often overestimated the size of the Southern forces.

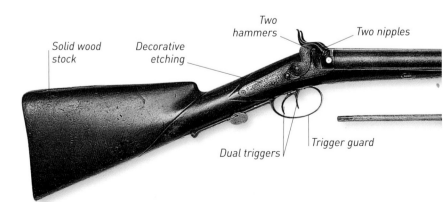

Solid wood stock · Decorative etching · Two hammers · Two nipples · Trigger guard · Dual triggers

Mosby's Partisan Rangers attack

Mosby was well-known to Northerners because Union newspapers carried stories about the "Gray Ghost." He and his troops were famous for attacking Union soldiers and then slipping away without a trace. This newspaper drawing shows an assault by Mosby's men on a Union army wagon.

Wood defensive walls

Guard towers

Fortified wood gates

A socialite spy

Young widow Rose O'Neal Greenhow was a socialite and Confederate spy. She threw parties for Union leaders who discussed war business in front of her. Eventually, she was caught and sent to Washington's Old Capitol Prison. This photograph of Mrs. Greenhow and her daughter was taken there.

Protecting a bridge

Saboteurs, people who destroy enemy equipment, found wooden military bridges easy to burn down. Union troops protected their bridges by fortifying them with walls and putting gates and guard towers at both ends.

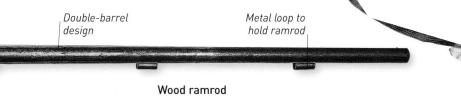

Double-barrel design

Metal loop to hold ramrod

Wood ramrod

A guerrilla favorite

Shotguns were popular weapons with guerrillas. A shotgun packed as much punch as a pistol and could hit more than one soldier at a time. The weapon shown here is a 12-gauge muzzle loader carried by a Confederate.

March to the Sea

Union Major General William T. Sherman's campaign to capture Atlanta was the first step in his plan to crush Georgia. In the summer of 1864, Sherman penned Southern forces in Atlanta, then forced them to abandon it. His troops rested there from September 2 to November 12, then burned much of the city to the ground. His men then marched west to Savannah on Georgia's Atlantic coast. All along their route, the soldiers burned towns, leaving civilians homeless and hungry. Sherman said he wanted "to make all Georgia howl." He did. When the Union army arrived in Savannah, the Confederates could not resist and surrendered after a 15-minute fight. On December 21, Savannah's Confederate commander, General Hardee, had his troops leave the city. Union troops paraded through the streets, celebrating their victory.

General Oliver O. Howard
General John Logan
General William T. Sherman
General Henry Slocum

Sherman and his officers

This photograph shows General Sherman and his generals. General Logan helped establish the holiday now known as Memorial Day to honor those killed in the Civil War.

The city of Atlanta is conquered

This home was built on the outskirts of Atlanta. Unfortunately for its owner, it sat right along the Confederate army's main defense line and was riddled by Union cannon fire.

Atlanta's railroads destroyed

Confederate General John Hood commanded the troops inside Atlanta. As he retreated from the city, he had his men destroy Atlanta's railroad roundhouse and burn the railroad cars.

Fake guns

Sherman's men ran into small Confederate fortifications along the March to the Sea. Sometimes the forts' "cannons" were actually logs that had been cut and painted to look as though they were big guns from a distance. This painting shows Union soldiers surprised at discovering that they were only threatened by logs.

An aging draftee

Danish immigrant Charles Stevens settled in Savannah with his family before the war. At 48, he was considered too old to serve in the Confederate army; but as Sherman's army neared, Stevens was pressed into a local militia unit. He was captured by Union soldiers and died in a prisoner-of-war camp.

Demolished home

This picture of Union soldiers resting among the rubble of a Georgia house was taken outside Atlanta. The destruction is remarkable. Even the window frames are removed. There are no known photographs of similar destruction along the March to the Sea. The Northern army moved too rapidly for slow, nineteenth-century cameras.

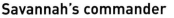

Savannah's commander

Confederate General William J. Hardee commanded the soldiers inside the city of Savannah. Although his few troops could not possibly have won against Sherman's large force, the defeat tarnished his military reputation.

A victory parade through Savannah

This sketch shows Sherman's victory parade through Savannah. Union soldiers spared this attractive old city.

The Confederacy surrenders

Grant's army besieged Lee's forces at Petersburg, Virginia, from June 1864 until April 1865. In December 1864, Confederate General Hood's army was crushed at Nashville, Tennessee. Then, on April 1, 1865, Union troops overran Confederates in the Battle of Five Forks near Petersburg. Confederate officials abandoned nearby Richmond, and Lee's army retreated to Appomytox Court House, Virginia. Grant's forces surrounded Lee's there, and on April 9, General Lee surrendered. Soon afterward, Confederate generals Johnston, Smith, and Watie surrendered. This put an informal end to America's deadliest war.

Officers standing out of rifle range

In the trenches at war's end
In the last months of the war, Union and Confederate soldiers fought from trenches. These Union troops are resting behind trench lines before moving forward to resume fighting.

Jubilant slaves *U.S.C.T. regiment* *Scavengers*

Meeting in peace
Officers of Sherman's and Johnston's armies mingle around the North Carolina home of James Bennett, the site of their generals' surrender negotiations. These talks continued for several days while terms were discussed.

Union troops in the Confederate capital
When President Jefferson Davis and his officials fled Richmond, panic broke out. The capital was already a burning wreck when the black Union troops shown in this illustration walked into the city.

Where the war ended
Four years of bloody civil war came to an end in the tiny parlor of Wilmer McClean's house. It was there that Lee signed a surrender document prepared by Grant.

The South in ruins

The war ended with entire Southern cities destroyed by fire. Many thousands of people were homeless, and there was little food to be had. This photograph shows the destruction in Columbia, the capital of South Carolina.

Lee in defeat

After his meeting with Grant, Robert E. Lee packed his belongings and rode away alone to find his family. A few days later, he put on his Confederate uniform one last time and posed on the back porch of the house his wife had rented in Richmond.

Union Lieutenant Colonel Eli Parker, Grant's military secretary

Union General Ulysses S. Grant

Confederate General Robert E. Lee

Union Major General Philip Sheridan

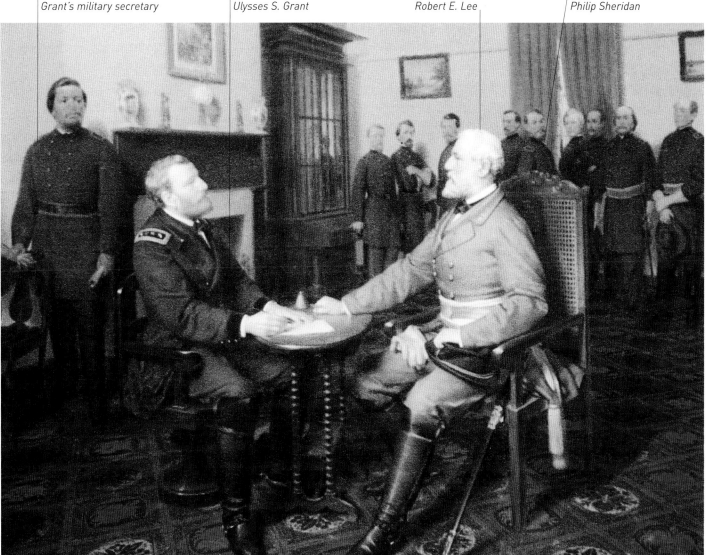

Two military leaders meet

Surrounded by Union troops near the village of Appomattox Court House, General Lee sent a note to General Grant. In it, he asked for surrender terms. Grant met Lee in a nearby house just outside the hamlet and there accepted the surrender of the Confederate army. Lee's troops were allowed to find their own way home. In addition, his officers could keep their horses and sidearms.

The fates of two leaders

Within days of Lee's surrender, the Union lost its leader. On April 14, 1865, President Abraham Lincoln went to Ford's Theatre in Washington, D.C., with his wife and friends Clara Harris and Major Henry Rathbone. An actor named John Wilkes Booth slipped behind the president's seat and shot him in the back of the head. When Rathbone went after Booth, the assassin slashed him with a knife, then escaped on horseback. Lincoln died the next morning. On April 24, Booth was killed in a barn in Virginia. Several of his associates were arrested for helping him with the plot. Meanwhile, US troops were searching for Confederate President Jefferson Davis. He and his cabinet members had fled from Richmond on April 2. Weeks later, Davis was captured near Irwinville, Georgia. By May 22, Davis was imprisoned at Fort Monroe, Virginia, and remained there for two years.

The assassin
John Wilkes Booth was a famous actor in his day. Thousands of his fans were shocked at his attack on Lincoln. They were not aware of Booth's strong Confederate sympathies.

Crime scene
Ford's Theatre, where Abraham Lincoln was killed, was owned by John Ford. He and many actors who knew Booth were held by the authorities after the murder, and the theater was closed. Today the building is a National Historic Landmark.

Davis in custody
Jefferson Davis's wife and family were with him when he was captured. They and other members of their party were placed in ambulances and driven into Macon, Georgia. This is the only known photograph of the group in custody. His family did not see or hear from him until many months later.

Davis's last flag
This Confederate battle flag was carried by Jefferson Davis's military escort during his flight from US troops. He and his party were seized in Georgia one night while they were gathered around a campfire. Not a shot was fired.

The murder
After the shooting, the unconscious president was carried across the street from the theater to the small home of a tailor named Petersen. Lincoln passed away there near dawn the next day.

Knife used to slash Major Rathbone

Booth's single-shot derringer

Playing at Ford's Theatre
The president was watching a performance of *Our American Cousin*, starring Laura Keene. She knew Booth, but had no part in the plot to kill the president.

Mary Todd Lincoln

Major Henry Rathbone

Clara Harris

Another plot member
This is a police mug shot of Lewis Powell, alias Lewis Paine. As Booth was shooting Lincoln, Powell was attacking Secretary of State William Seward. That murder attempt was not successful. Powell was convicted of helping Booth and hanged.

In prison
Jefferson Davis was held in a dank dungeon cell in Fort Monroe, Virginia. For a long time, he was manacled to an iron ball and chain. His case never went to trial. After two years, Davis was bailed out of prison with funds raised by Northern newspaper publisher Horace Greeley.

A conspirator
Mary Surratt ran a boardinghouse in Washington, D.C., where the conspirators often met. She was convicted of taking part in the plot and was the first woman ever executed by the federal government.

Handcuffs

A life of freedom

Cheers for Lincoln
On April 5, 1865, President Lincoln toured the newly conquered Confederate capital of Richmond, Virginia. He was cheered by newly freed black men and women. Although the president had issued his final Emancipation Proclamation two years before, the ex-slaves had only recently learned of it.

After more than two hundred years of bondage, America's slaves were freed when the Thirteenth Amendment to the US Constitution was passed in December, 1865. Across the South, black Americans wandered the countryside looking for a new start. To deal with these estimated four million people, the government set up the Freedmen's Bureau, an agency that housed, fed, and educated refugees. Meanwhile, opportunistic Northerners called Carpetbaggers tried to gain the political support of freedmen, who now had voting rights. Many ex-slaves returned to their former masters' plantations and worked there again as poorly paid employees. Others helped rebuild the South to make it a good home for their families.

Free at last
Most slaves in the Deep South did not know of Lincoln's Emancipation Proclamation until Union forces came to their communities and read the document to them. This artwork shows a black Union trooper reading out the proclamation to newly freed men and women.

Military-style tunic

Settlement
This settlement for homeless ex-slaves looks like an army barracks. Many of these first refugee "villages" were built by government laborers. Later, the Freedmen's Bureau hired refugees to do some of the building themselves.

A symbol of freedom
This unidentified freedman had his photograph taken in a studio in Louisiana. It was a victory for civil rights that a Southern black man could walk into a white photographer's studio and pay for his picture, just as a white patron would.

Unemployed
These South Carolina slaves are free, but they are without a means of supporting themselves. Some plantation owners ran away from advancing Union armies and left their slaves without food or clothing. But in the months after the war, former slaves and slave owners sometimes reunited, working together as employers and employees.

Lynching victim

Terrors of the night
After the war, groups of hooded night riders terrorized ex-slaves, Carpetbaggers, and sympathetic Southerners. The lynchings and beatings that they carried out were documented in the Northern press with drawings such as this one. The Ku Klux Klan ignored calls from many ex-Confederates to disband and set itself up as a violent underground government in the postwar South.

Threatening a free family
When freedmen were given the right to vote, some former Confederates organized themselves into terrorist bands to intimidate them. The Ku Klux Klan was the most famous of these groups.

A new era begins

A popular president
Despite several financial scandals within his administration, Ulysses S. Grant was always popular with the public. His vision of America's future was farsighted. While touring the South in the 1870s, he thanked black church members for their support and talked of their place in politics.

For more than ten years after the Civil War, the South was occupied by federal troops. This period in US history is known as Reconstruction. Those who had served in the Confederate army had to take an oath of allegiance to enjoy some of the benefits of citizenship. Some never regained the right to vote. Meanwhile, newly freed slaves were encouraged to vote in local elections. Several African Americans were appointed to federal and local government positions, and some became members of the US House of Representatives. Ambitious Carpetbaggers moved into the South, buying out businesses and taking over local government positions. Southerners who cooperated with the Carpetbaggers were called Scalawags. Elected president in 1868, Ulysses S. Grant served two terms and presided over the nation's industrial expansion. And in 1876, the United States celebrated its centennial. Many of the festivities were held in Philadelphia, Pennsylvania, the nation's birthplace.

A veteran's orphans
No story explained the healing between North and South better than the tale of General John Bell Hood's children. At the end of the war, Hood had lost a leg and the use of one arm. Despite his disabilities, Hood married and fathered many children, including three sets of twins. In the 1870s, he, his wife, and their oldest child died of yellow fever. Confederate veterans circulated this photograph of Hood's surviving children, looking for adoptive parents. All of the Hood orphans were adopted—by families from the North as well as the South.

General John Bell Hood

John C. Breckinridge

Southerners in exile
This group of ex-Confederates fled to Canada after the Civil War. One of these men, John C. Breckinridge, was a former Confederate general. Neither he nor the other men with him were punished for having taken part in the conflict. Breckinridge later returned to the US and became governor of Kentucky.

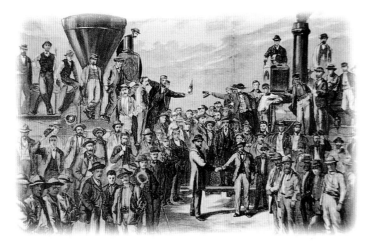

United nation

This painting commemorates the joining of the Union Pacific and Central Pacific railroads at Promontory Point, Utah, in 1869. Railroad officials completed the first transcontinental railroad by connecting the last rails with a gold spike.

A soldier's funeral

Robert E. Lee died in 1870 at the age of 63. This is a photograph of his funeral ceremony. In his later years, Lee was praised in the North because he encouraged Southerners to embrace peace and to respect the role of free blacks in American society.

Washington College's chapel

The great centennial

Independence Day, 1876, marked America's centennial (one hundredth birthday). There was a great fair in Philadelphia, where all the marvels of technology were displayed. Machines like the great Corliss engine (above) promised work and prosperity for the reunited American people.

Saxhorn   *Bass drum*   *Louisiana state flag*   *US flag*

Carpetbag politics

In the postwar years, a political candidate would have a band travel around a community in a wagon, playing for the public and gathering support for him. This Carpetbagger candidate's bandwagon was used during a campaign in Louisiana.

Did you know?

FASCINATING FACTS

⭐ Although both the North and the South outlawed enlisting women in the army, historians estimate that 250 to 400 female soldiers fought in the Civil War disguised as men.

⭐ The reward for the capture of Harriet Tubman is said to have been $40,000—that is over half a million dollars in today's money.

⭐ At the start of the war, the Union army had two horse-drawn ambulances and few tools, and the South had even less equipment. Reports claim that after the First Battle of Bull Run, no wounded soldiers reached Washington, D.C., by ambulance, but some walked the 27 miles (43 km) for help.

Zouave troops learning to load wounded soldiers into an ambulance

⭐ Before reading the Emancipation Proclamation to his cabinet, Lincoln read an essay from *Artemus Ward: His Book*. It included an imagined interview with Lincoln himself.

⭐ The last Southern troops surrendered on May 26, 1865. Shortly afterward, survivors began decorating the graves of those who had died in the war. They repeated the ritual each year on "Decoration Day"—now known as Memorial Day.

⭐ Three future presidents of the United States fought in the Civil War: Ulysses S. Grant, Rutherford B. Hayes, and William McKinley.

⭐ Some Southerners objected to slavery on moral grounds; others political. In 1857, North Carolinian Hinton R. Helper argued in his book *The Impending Crisis* that slavery gave too much power to planters, at the expense of non-slave-owning whites.

⭐ When large numbers of Union volunteers arrived in Washington, D.C., at the start of the war, there were not enough barracks to hold them. Some Kansas volunteers stayed in the East Room of the White House; Massachusetts soldiers camped in the Capitol building.

⭐ At the end of the war, 60,000 Union soldiers were missing. President Lincoln asked Clara Barton, founder of the American Red Cross, to help find out what had happened to them. She accounted for 22,000 soldiers.

⭐ Huge mortars used in the war could pitch a 200-lb (91-kg) cannonball over a distance of 2½ miles (4 km).

⭐ George B. McClellan, who was fired by President Lincoln, ran against Abraham Lincoln for the presidency in 1864. He lost, but was later elected governor of New Jersey.

⭐ The most common operation performed by surgeons in the Civil War was amputation. With little or no pain relief, the most a patient could hope for was a quick operation. The best surgeons could have a limb severed within five minutes.

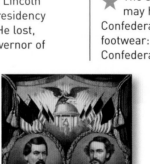
A broadside promoting George B. McClellan

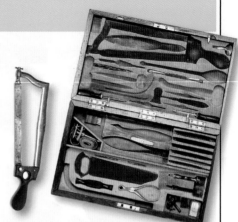
The amputation saw and tool kit of a field surgeon

⭐ Though Virginia was home to the Confederacy's capital, it had relatively few slaveholders: 2,184 out of more than one million Virginians.

⭐ Ulysses S. Grant was so tone deaf that he liked to say he could only recognize two tunes: "One is Yankee Doodle and the other one isn't."

⭐ General Lee opposed both slavery and secession, but agreed to lead the Confederate Army out of loyalty to his home state of Virginia.

⭐ In an average day during the Civil War, about 600 people were killed. By the end of the war, more than 618,000 people had died.

⭐ The site of the Battle of Gettysburg may have been influenced by Confederate soldiers' dire need for footwear: the day before fighting began, Confederate troops headed to the town on a mission for shoes.

⭐ The youngest soldier in the Civil War was a nine-year-old boy from Mississippi. The oldest was an 80-year-old from Iowa.

⭐ Poet Walt Whitman was a nurse in the Civil War.

⭐ Edward Everett, the headline speaker at the Gettysburg dedication, talked for two hours; Lincoln spoke for about two minutes. His speech made history.

QUESTIONS AND ANSWERS

Q Did the Emancipation Proclamation end slavery?

A Not exactly. The Emancipation Proclamation was made up of two orders: In the first, President Lincoln ordered that in all states still in rebellion by January 1, 1863, slaves would be declared free. On January 1,1863, the second order named ten Confederate states where the order applied—but exempted some areas. Though it freed existing slaves, the Proclamation did not actually outlaw slavery anywhere.

Emancipation Proclamation

Q What happened to runaway slaves during the Civil War?

A Slaves who ran away sometimes found sanctuary with Union soldiers, but their masters could track them down and demand their return under the Fugitive Slave Act. At Union-occupied Fort Monroe in Virginia, Major General Benjamin Butler refused to return the runaways. The runaway slaves became a useful workforce for the Union and more than 10,000 African Americans stayed at the fort during the war.

Q Did all Southerners own slaves before the war?

A No—most Southerners were not slaveholders. Less than a quarter of whites there had any direct connection to slavery. However, African Americans accounted for more than a third of the total population of the South.

Q Were African Americans subject to the draft?

A In the North, African Americans were subject to the Union draft. In border states, slaves could be drafted, too; slaveholders were paid for each slave who joined the army. But commanders often kept African Americans busy on building projects or other work, rather than sending them to the front lines.

Q Who fired the first shots in the Civil War?

A At Fort Sumter, the war began with shots fired by Edmund Ruffin, a Virginia planter and slaveholder, and New York-born Abner Doubleday, who later was credited (most say falsely) with inventing baseball.

Q In Civil War equestrian statues, is there meaning in the position of the hooves?

A Many believe that a horse's position in a statue is code for the fate of its rider: One leg up means the rider was wounded in battle; two legs up means he was killed in battle; four legs on the ground means he survived. However, it is generally an unreliable guide.

An equestrian statue of Robert E. Lee

Q Did any Southerners vote for Lincoln for president?

A Not many. In the presidential election of 1860, Abraham Lincoln received 0 popular votes in 9 of the 13 slave states. (In Virginia, he managed to eke out 1 percent of the votes.) Most Southerners supported Southern Democrat John Breckinridge or John Bell of the Constitutional Union party. Not a single Southern vote went to Lincoln during his reelection campaign of 1864.

Q Why was Mathew Brady important to history?

A Photographer Mathew Brady is often called the first "photojournalist"— and was one of the pioneering photographers who made the Civil War the first war to be photographed. In truth, Brady spent much of his time organizing the operation from Washington, D.C. He hired 23 photographers to work for him.

Mathew Brady

Runaway slaves working at Fort Monroe

Timeline

Both North and South entered the war expecting a quick victory for their side. Instead, tensions that had been building for decades exploded into a bloody, years-long conflict, made up of over 50 major battles.

Fighting at the Second Battle of Bull Run

THE SECOND BATTLE OF BULL RUN, FOUGHT AUG? 29TH 1862.

A slave ship's cramped quarters

1619 The first African slaves to reach America arrive in Virginia.

1807 Importation of slaves is outlawed.

1820 Missouri Compromise: Maintains a balance of free and slave states.

1850 Compromise of 1850: Allows new states to decide for themselves whether to be slave states or free states.

1852 *Uncle Tom's Cabin* is published, exposing the cruelty of slavery.

1857 Supreme Court rules that slaves are not US citizens and are not protected by the Constitution. Congress has no authority to outlaw slavery.

October 1859 John Brown and his men raid an arsenal at Harpers Ferry, Virginia, to arm slaves.

November 1860 Abraham Lincoln is elected president.

December 20, 1860 South Carolina secedes from the Union.

Illustration from Beecher Stowe's *Uncle Tom's Cabin*

February 1861 Representatives from Alabama, Florida, Georgia, Louisiana, Mississippi, and South Carolina meet in Montgomery, Alabama, to form the Confederate States of America. Later, they are joined by Virginia, Texas, North Carolina, Tennessee, and Arkansas.

April 12, 1861 Fort Sumter is attacked, and the Civil War begins. *CSA victory*

July 21, 1861 First Battle of Bull Run. *CSA victory*

February 6, 1862 Fall of Fort Henry. *Union victory*

February 16, 1862 Surrender of Fort Donelson. *Union victory*

March 9, 1862 Battle of the *Monitor* and the *Virginia. Draw*

April 6–7, 1862 Battle of Shiloh. *Union victory*

April 25, 1862 Fall of New Orleans. *Union victory*

May 31–June 1, 1862 Battle of Seven Pines. *Inconclusive*

June 26–July 2, 1862 The Seven Days Battles. *CSA victory*

August 29–30, 1862 Second Battle of Bull Run. *CSA victory*

September 17, 1862 Battle of Antietam (Sharpsburg). *Inconclusive*

September 22, 1862 The Emancipation Proclamation declares all slaves in areas persisting in rebellion to be free.

December 13, 1862 Battle of Fredericksburg. *CSA victory*

December 31, 1862–January 2, 1863 Battle of Stones River. *Inconclusive*

January 1, 1863 The Emancipation Proclamation declares slaves in 10 named states to be free (although some areas are exempted).

May 1–6, 1863 Battle of Chancellorsville. *CSA victory*

May 18–July 4, 1863 Siege of Vicksburg. *Union victory*

July 1–3, 1863 Battle of Gettysburg. *Union victory*

September 19–20, 1863 Battle of Chickamauga. *CSA victory*

Lee at the Battle of Chancellorsville

November 19, 1863 Lincoln delivers Gettysburg Address.

November 23–25, 1863 Battle of Chattanooga. *Union victory*

May 5–6, 1864 Battle of the Wilderness. *Inconclusive*

May 8–12, 1864 Battle of Spotsylvania. *Inconclusive*

May 11, 1864 Battle of Yellow Tavern. *Union victory*

June 3, 1864 Battle of Cold Harbor. *CSA victory*

June 18, 1864 Siege of Petersburg begins. *Union victory*

August 5, 1864 Farragut enters Mobile Bay. *Union victory*

September 2, 1864 Fall of Atlanta. *Union victory*

November 8, 1864 Lincoln is reelected to the presidency.

November 15, 1864 Sherman's March to the Sea begins.

November 30, 1864 Battle of Franklin. *Union victory*

Siege of Vicksburg

December 15–16, 1864 Battle of Nashville. *Union victory*

February 1, 1864 The Thirteenth Amendment proposed, outlawing slavery.

March 1865 Congress establishes the Freedmen's Bureau to help freed slaves.

April 2, 1865 Fall of Petersburg and Richmond. *Union victory*

April 9, 1865 Lee surrenders at Appomattox. *Union victory*

April 15, 1865 Lincoln is assassinated by John Wilkes Booth. Vice President Andrew Johnson becomes president.

1865 The Ku Klux Klan is formed.

December 1865 The Thirteenth Amendment, prohibiting slavery, is ratified.

April 1866 The Civil Rights Act is passed.

1866 The Fourteenth Amendment is approved. It guarantees all people born, or naturalized, in America citizenship and equal protection in law.

July 30, 1866 New Orleans Race Riot.

1867 The First, Second, and Third Reconstruction Acts are passed.

1868 Oscar J. Dunn, a former slave, is elected lieutenant governor of Louisiana.

1868 The Fourth Reconstruction Act is passed.

1868 The Fourteenth Amendment is ratified.

1868 John Menard of Louisiana becomes the first African American representative to speak on the floor of the House.

1869 Ulysses S. Grant becomes president.

1870 Hiram Rhodes Revels of Mississippi becomes the first African American member of the U.S. Senate.

1879 The last federal troops leave South Carolina, ending the Federal government's presence in the South.

Robert E. Lee surrendering to Ulysses S. Grant at Appomattox Court House, Virginia

Find out more

For many Americans, a journey into Civil War history is just a car trip away. Battlefields, monuments, and historic homes are open to visitors in many parts of the country. For those who live far from the sites, a fascinating array of websites brings the Civil War to life online.

Museums

Plan a trip to a museum to view letters, weapons, and medical equipment. The African American Civil War Memorial and Museum in Washington, D.C., houses photographs, documents, and audio-visual equipment to help visitors understand the role of African Americans in their fight for freedom.

Historic homes

Walking into a historic home can give you the feel of Civil War times in an instant. Some houses played key roles in the war: In Appomattox Court House, Virginia, the McLean House (above) was where General Robert E. Lee surrendered to General Ulysses S. Grant.

Reenactments

Search online to find a reenactment near you, and watch as actors in period costumes portray Civil War battles. Weapons, uniforms, and actual battle formations are reproduced to look and sound as they did in the original conflict.

USEFUL WEBSITES

• Discover interactive battle maps, guides to weapons and ships, and a history of slavery: **www.civilwar.com**

• Find photos, activities, and a Civil War timeline: **www.Americancivilwar. com/kids_zone/**

• Learn about the role of women in the Civil War: **www.history.com/ topics/american-civil-war/women-in-the-civil-war**

• Gain an insight into the Civil War: **www.history.com/topics/american-civil-war/civil-war-culture**

• Look at battle summaries, maps, and biographies: **www.pbs.org/ civilwar/war/**

• Get an overview of the Civil War: **www.civilwar.org/education/history/ civil-war-overview/overview.html**

• Find more Civil War facts: **www.historynet.com/civil-war**

Union soldier's discharge papers

Soldiers in your family

Some websites offer databases of Civil War soldiers. Enter a name to discover whether your ancestors played a role. Try **www.itd.nps.gov/cwss**.

National military parks

Search the National Parks Service website (www.nps.gov) for a military park in your state. Each has something unique to offer: a stunning number of monuments and markers (as pictured at Gettysburg, above), unusual artifacts (such as the pencil used by Robert E. Lee to surrender documents at Appomattox Court House), and more. Start with the visitors' center, and ask for a NPS Junior Ranger booklet with activities and information for kids.

Civil War cemeteries

Walking through a Civil War cemetery can be both moving and serene. Bring along a crayon and paper to make a rubbing of some of the headstones you find.

PLACES TO VISIT

GETTYSBURG, PENNSYLVANIA

Tour the vast battlefield and its 1,328 statues, and see tents and gear displayed just as they would have looked in camp.

ANTIETAM, MARYLAND

See some of the more than 500 cannons used during the battle of Antietam on a self-guided auto tour or hike.

NATIONAL MUSEUM OF CIVIL WAR MEDICINE, MARYLAND

Learn about the courage, science, and luck behind battlefield surgery and medicine and visit the five "immersion exhibits."

VICKSBURG, MISSISSIPPI

Visit the country's largest burial ground of Civil War dead, take a battlefield tour, and check out the ironclad USS *Cairo*.

JOHN RANKIN HOUSE, RIPLEY, OHIO

Walk in the footsteps of the 2,000 slaves who passed through this house on the Underground Railroad.

MUSEUM OF THE CONFEDERACY, RICHMOND, VIRGINIA

View the world's largest collection of Confederate artifacts.

Glossary

ABOLITIONIST A supporter of outlawing, or abolishing, slavery.

AMPUTATION Cutting off a wounded or infected body part, such as an arm or leg.

ARTILLERY Mortars, cannons, or other large guns, or the military units who used them.

BARRACKS A simple building or group of buildings used for housing soldiers.

BAYONET A blade designed to attach to the end of a musket or rifle.

BLANKET ROLL A leather covering used to protect a blanket, either fixed on top of a knapsack or carried with a strap.

BLOCKADE A tactic to prevent supplies or information from reaching a country's ports, as the Union navy did to Southern ports during the war.

BLOCKADE RUNNER A boat used to slip through an enemy's blockade in order to transport weapons, food, and commercial trade.

BONE SAW A medical instrument used to cut through bone.

Bayonet

BORDER STATE A slave state that did not secede and whose citizens were split between support of the North and South; at the beginning of the war: Delaware, Kentucky, Maryland, Missouri, and West Virginia.

BOUNTY A payment offered to encourage volunteers to enlist in the army.

BOWIE KNIFE A knife with a blade as long as a man's forearm.

BULLET MOLD A device for making bullets out of melted lead.

BUTTERNUT A nickname for a Confederate soldier, taken from the nut-brown color of the home-dyed uniforms that became common late in the war.

CANNON A large field artillery weapon made up of a bronze or steel tube, from which cannonballs are fired using explosives.

CANTEEN A container for holding drinking water, often made of metal and covered in canvas.

Case shot

CARPETBAGGER A Northerner who traveled through the South after the war, seeking political or financial gain.

CASE SHOT An artillery round made of one larger "case" and a smaller shot within.

CAVALRY Troops who went into battle on horseback, carrying swords or sabers.

CONFEDERACY The seceded Southern states.

CONFEDERATE STATES OF AMERICA (CSA) The name chosen by the secessionist Southern states for their new nation and government, which valued states' rights, an agricultural economy, and the continuation of slavery.

CONSCRIPTION The draft; being called to serve in the military without having volunteered.

COTTON GIN A mechanical device that removed seeds from cotton, greatly increasing the amount of cotton a plantation could prepare for sale.

EMANCIPATION The act of freeing slaves.

ESPIONAGE Spying; secretly gathering information about an enemy's plans to use against them.

FEDERALS Supporters of the Union cause, or soldiers in the Union army.

Cotton gin

FIRE-EATERS A prewar name for supporters of secession.

FREE STATE A state where slavery was illegal.

FREEDMEN Former slaves who were freed by the end of the Civil War.

FREEDMEN'S BUREAU The government organization established to assist former slaves by providing housing, food, and education.

GUERILLA An individual who uses unusual or unofficial tactics when fighting an enemy army.

HARDTACK A hard biscuit given as part of a Union soldier's rations.

HAVERSACK A shoulder bag used to carry rations and personal effects.

INFANTRY Troops who went into battle on foot, carrying firearms.

IRONCLAD A warship plated with iron as a defense against enemy fire.

Canteen and haversack

KEPI A small, visored cap with a crown that dips lower at the front.

KU KLUX KLAN A postwar terrorist group founded to intimidate African Americans and discourage carpetbaggers.

LEG IRON A type of restraint used in slave auctions and slave importation, or for punishment.

MEDAL OF HONOR The highest honor given for bravery by the US government.

Ironclad warships *Monitor* and *Virginia*

MILITIA Citizen-soldiers activated during a crisis.

MINE An explosive device set to explode on contact or by a remote trigger.

MORTAR A launching device, similar to a cannon, used to launch shells high over enemy fortifications.

MUZZLE The firing end of a gun.

PECULIAR INSTITUTION The South's name for the institution of slavery.

PLANTATION A family homestead with farms and fields, often reliant in pre-Civil War times on slave labor to handle the work of planting and harvesting cotton, tobacco, and other crops.

QUAKER GUNS Fake guns made of logs or other materials to fool the enemy.

RAMROD A device used to push ammunition into a gun before firing.

RATIONS The daily servings of food alotted by the army to each soldier.

RECONSTRUCTION A period after the Civil War when the federal government occupied the South, in an attempt to bring its former enemies back in line with the Union and prevent further rebellion.

REVOLVER A handgun, usually worn in a holster, designed to fire bullets from a revolving barrel.

RIFLED A gun barrel that is cut or grooved on the inside to help guide the path of a bullet or cannonball.

SABER A curved sword often used by cavalrymen.

SCALAWAG Southern slang for those who collaborated with carpetbaggers.

SECESSION Formal withdrawal from an united group or government.

SHACKLES Iron restraints used to prevent slaves from running away.

SIEGE An attempt to force an enemy to surrender by cutting off supplies.

SLAVE AUCTION The sale of enslaved people to the highest bidder.

SLAVE STATE A state where slavery was legal.

Cavalry saber

SMOOTHBORE A gun barrel that is smooth or uncut on the inside, allowing for greater variety of ammunition but less accuracy.

TORPEDO An underwater explosive weapon. (*see* MINE.)

TRENCH A ditch cut into the ground for the defense of soldiers.

UNDERGROUND RAILROAD A secret system of people and locations that cooperated to help escaped slaves make their way to Northern states and to Canada.

U.S.C.T. US Colored Troops; segregated military units that fought for the Union.

ZOUAVE A soldier in flamboyant dress taken from the style of some French regiments, which in turn was modeled after the Zouava tribe in Africa.

Zouave uniform

Index

Acknowledgments

The author and DK Publishing wish to thank: Confederate Memorial Hall, New Orleans, LA; Gettysburg National Military Park, Gettysburg, PA; Old Capitol Museum of Mississippi, Jackson, MS; US Army Military History Institute, Carlisle, PA; William Penn Museum, Pennsylvania State Museum Commission, Harrisburg, PA; Louisiana State Museum, New Orleans, LA; National Civil War Museum, Harrisburg, PA; Herb Peck, Jr.; Joe Baughman; Lloyd Ostendorf; Cincinnati Museum of Art, Cincinnati, OH; Massachusetts Historical Society, Boston, MA; Chicago Historical Society, Chicago, IL; and Corbis Images, New York, NY. Image colorization provided by Slimfilms, New York, NY.

For this relaunch edition:
The publisher would like to thank Hazel Beynon for text editing and Carron Brown for proofreading.

Photography Credits:
[Key t=top; b=bottom; l=left; r=right; c=center]

Collection of Joseph Baughman 35t. **Bettman Corbis** 70tl. Demetrio Carrasco © Dorling Kindersley, Courtesy Gettysburg National Military Park 65tr. *Century Magazine* 26bl, 26tr, 46l, 63tr. **Chicago Historical Society** 6tc, 9t. *Civil War Times Illustrated* Collection Prints 6tl, 6bl, 15tl, 15b, 17cl, 18bl, 21tr, 21trc, 23br, 27t, 30bc, 33tr, 35bl, 35br, 36tl, 36c, 39bl, 40tr, 41tl, 43cl, 43tr. **Confederate Memorial Hall, New Orleans, LA** 14t, 14lc, 15r, 16rc, 17lc, 23rc, 24tl, 24lc, 24lbc, 27lc, 27rc, 28tl, 28bl, 29rc, 30rc, 31tr, 32tl, 32lc, 33br, 34br, 36blc, 37tl, 37tr, 37c, 37bl, 38br, 38bl, 38c, 39tr, 39trc, 40tl, 40rc, 40lc, 41tr, 42bl, 43tl, 49tl, 49rc, 49b, 50lc, 50br, 51rc, 52rc, 52- 53bc, 61rc, 62lc, 62bl. **Barnaby Conrad Collection, Carpenteria, CA** 52bl. **Corbis** 6bc, 12tr, 13bl, 13br, 13tr, 18br, 19lc, 20c, 21br, 23bl, 25l, 30lc, 31lc, 31bc, 35lc, 38-39rc, 40bl, 47tl, 52bl, 54tc, 54bc, 56tr, 57l, 57br, 58cr, 59tr, 59br, 60b, 61bl, 61bl, 62tl, 63tl. **William C. Davis Collection** 62br. *Frank Leslie's Illustrated Newspaper* 14b, 16b, 17b, 26-27bc, 34c, 42lc, 44bl, 45tr, 50-51tc, 51lcb, 53, 56lc, 56lb, 60tl. **Gettysburg**
National Military Park 16-17tc, 24brc, 24b, 29t, 32cb, 32b, 33tr, 33trc, 33rc, 36tr, 36b, 37br, 39bl, 39br, 40-41bc, 41tl, 41tlc, 41tr, 45tl, 45br, 50ct, 50cb. **Jack G. Grothe Collection** 19bl. **John O. Hess** 22br. **Illinois State Historical Association** 32tr. **International Museum of Photography, Rochester, NY** 33br. **Kansas State Historical Society** 7br. Dave King © Dorling Kindersley, Courtesy of the Gettysburg National Military Park, PA 64tr, 70tr, 71l, 71br. Dave King © Dorling Kindersley, Courtesy of the US Army Heritage and Education Center - Military History Institute 70rc. **Library of Congress** 7t, 7bl, 11bl, 19r, 22br, 26c, 29bc, 33bl, 46tr, 48c, 49cl, 49tr, 50tr, 51br, 54bl, 55br, 58tr, 61bl, 64cl, 64br, 65tl, 65bl, 65br, 66tl, 66bl, 67tc, 68bl, 69tl, 69tr, 71t. **Lincoln Museum, Harrowgate, TN** 34l. **Louisiana Historical Association** 25r. **Louisiana State Museum** 8tr, 8bl. **Department of Archives & Manuscripts, Louisiana State University** 63b. **Commonwealth of Massachusetts** 19tcr. **Massachusetts Historical Society** 12tl. Collection of Michael J. McAfee 18-19rc. **State Archives of Michigan** 21c. **National Archives** 10tr, 11br, 14tr, 19br, 50bc, 53br, 58-59rc, 59bc, 59br. **The National Civil War Museum** 10r. **National Park Service** 57bl, 67bl, 68tr, 69bl, 69br. **National Portrait Gallery** 33tr, 33bl, 42tr. **Old Capitol Museum of Mississippi**
History 16cl, 36lc, 48bl. **Old Court House Museum, Vicksburg, MS** 44t. Ruth Koerner Oliver Collection 45bl. Gary Ombler © Dorling Kindersley, Courtesy of Southern Skirmish Association 70tl. Angus Osborn © Rough Guides 68cl. **Lloyd Ostendorf Collection** 10br, 20bl. **Charles E. Pearson Collection** 55tr. **Pennsylvania State Museum** 42- 43bc, 43cr, 44rc, 46-47bc, 47tr. **Fanny U. Phillips** 20rc. R.W. Norton Art Gallery, Shreveport, LA 66bl. **Marian B. Ralph Collection** 52lc. **Smithsonian Institution** 11t. Jacob Termansen and Pia Marie Molbech © Dorling Kindersley, Courtesy of Peter Keim 64-71bg. **Union League Club** 22tl. **US Army Military History Institute** 8c, 8-9c, 12bl, 12br, 21tl, 24tcr, 26c, 28br, 29tc, 29br, 53lc, 55lc, 58bl, 61c. **US Naval History Institute** 27br. **US Navy** 51bl. **Valentine Museum, Richmond, VA** 19rc, 30tl. **Vermont Historical Association** 34tl. **Library of Virginia** 48tl. **Washington & Lee University** 63c. **Kean Wilcox Collection** 23tl. **Collection of Shelby Young, Memphis, TN** 9tr.

All other images © Dorling Kindersley

For further information see:
www.dkimages.com